NATIVE AMERICAN
BEADWORK

NATIVE AMERICAN BEADWORK

William C. Orchard

DOVER PUBLICATIONS, INC.
Mineola, New York

Published in the United Kingdom by David & Charles, Brunel House, Forde Close, Newton Abbot, Devon TQ12 4PU.

Bibliographical Note

This Dover edition, first published in 2002, is an unabridged republication of the second edition of the work originally published by the Museum of the American Indian, Heye Foundation, New York, in 1975 under the title *Beads and Beadwork of the American Indians* (first publication: 1929). The 16 original color plates have been reproduced on the front, back, and inside covers. These plates also appear in black and white in their original positions in the book.

Library of Congress Cataloging-in-Publication Data

Orchard, William C.
    Native American beadwork / William C. Orchard.
        p. cm.
    Reprint. Originally published: New York : Museum of the American Indian, 1975.
    Includes bibliographical references.
    ISBN 0-486-42483-9 (pbk.)
    1. Indian beadwork—North America. 2. Indian beadwork. 3. Beads—America. 4. Indians—Clothing. I. Title.

E98.B46 O73 2002
745.58'2'08997—dc21

2002067622

Manufactured in the United States of America
Dover Publications, Inc., 31 East 2nd Street, Mineola, N.Y. 11501

To MRS. THEA HEYE

Through whose deep interest in the arts of the American Indian, and through whose generosity the Museum collections have been enriched with many of its finest examples of beadwork, this volume is respectfully dedicated by

The Author

CONTENTS

ILLUSTRATIONS

COLOR PLATES*

BLACK AND WHITE PLATES

* The original color plates have been reproduced in black and white on the pages indicated above. They also appear in full color on the front, back, and inside covers.

FIGURES

FOREWORD

F ROM its initial appearance in 1929, *Beads and Beadwork of the American Indians*[*] has become a classic reference book on the subject. Not only is it a technological study-in-depth; it also considers in greater detail than any other similar work the history, use, and distribution of New World beadwork art from prehistoric to modern times. It examines the variety of materials used, the design motifs of the finished product, and the role of early Europeans, whose colorful trade beads levied such a tremendous impact upon Indian economics and esthetics. It may be of interest to note that the scope of the volume, even at that early date, went beyond the limits of the term *American Indian,* as it was then commonly applied, to include the concept of the inhabitants of the entire Western Hemisphere—a concept which continues to be the tradition of this Museum to the present day.

William C. Orchard, a gifted artist, was born in England around 1865, came to the United States, worked for a short period at the American Museum of Natural History, and then entered the private employ of Dr. Heye. Upon the founding of the Museum of the American Indian in 1916, Mr. Orchard became preparator, continuing in this capacity until his retirement in 1935. He died in 1948. His genius in repairing and restoring specimens was remarkable, and he enjoyed a well-earned reputation throughout the museum world for his skill in creating models and dioramas of native scenes. His son, Fred, was also a preparator, serving on the staff of the Peabody Museum, Harvard University, for many years.

This book was originally published at a time when color photography was still in its infancy; due to the technology of the period, all of the original color plates were prepared from watercolor renderings by the author. For the present volume the specimens in these plates have been photographed anew. Most of the black-and-white plates have been processed from new negatives prepared especially for this reprint; some of the older negatives had entirely deteriorated, and a few specimens could not be located, requiring the rephotographing of the original plates. This accounts for the mixed quality of some of the reproductions.

13

* original title of the present volume

In reprinting this book, some minor errors have been corrected, but no effort has been made to rewrite the original text; the content remains essentially as the author left it. Happily, his closing paragraph has proven only partially true, and beadwork is still an active art today, albeit much less commonly practiced. It is, in fact, but one of several of the Indian art activities which have survived and even prospered in the half century since this study was made. It is perhaps more to the point to regret that the purpose for which most of the objects are created has undergone a major change, thereby weakening Native American cultural strength.

We are grateful to several members of the Museum staff for their untiring efforts in gathering together the many details necessary for this publication. Primary in these duties was the work of G. Lynette Miller, Registrar, who patiently collated the many specimens needed for photography. Carmelo Guadagno, Staff Photographer, prepared all of the new photographs; Ellenda Wulfestieg, Conservator, carefully repaired many of the older specimens; and Vincent Wilcox, Curator of the Research Branch, diligently searched out needed objects from the storage collection. Betty Borger undertook the task of editing the volume, and Arthur Fleisher went far beyond the usual call of duty in guiding the book through the printing processes. We acknowledge these several efforts with deepest appreciation, and we hope that the results will prove to be of continued reference value to all of our readers.

FREDERICK J. DOCKSTADER
Director

June 1975

INTRODUCTION

B EADS owe their origin to the desire by primitive man for personal adornment; but so ancient are they that attempts to trace their earliest sources have thus far been futile. So far as the New World is concerned, beads in a great variety of shapes and materials have been found on prehistoric sites almost everywhere, and some of them are undoubtedly of great age. It is therefore evident that early aborigines of the Western Hemisphere were quite familiar with the use of beads for purposes of adornment, in some cases as potent charms and in others as a medium of exchange. But many of the uses to which beads were put by early man can only be surmised. Their use was and is worldwide. It is my purpose in the present paper to treat the subject of beads as they were employed by the American Indians, with special reference to the technique of beadwork.

The accepted definition of a bead is " a little perforated ball of any suitable material intended to be strung with others and worn as an ornament, or used to form a rosary." Forms in as great a variety as the materials of which they are made have been found, so that the " little perforated ball " is only one of many forms included in the term. The prevailing conception of a bead, however, is that of an object with a central perforation; but in many instances the perforation does not occur centrally, hence it becomes difficult to differentiate beads from pendants. Indeed there are so many forms that, unless it is perfectly obvious that the object is other than a bead, it has been given the benefit of the doubt and classed as a bead.

Many of the older varieties of beads are extremely crude, some examples consisting merely of a suitably shaped stone or a pebble having a natural perforation, or a waterworn fragment of shell with either a natural or an artificial aperture. It is possible that some such objects may have been the earliest forms of beads. Other crude forms are those known as St. Cuthbert's beads, which are the single joints of the articulated stems of encrinites, a central perforation permitting them to be strung.

> " On a rock by Lindisform
> St. Cuthbert sits and toils to frame
> The sea-born beads that bear his name."

Many examples of crude beads have been found in association with others of exquisite workmanship, denoting that some of the former were in use after evident efficiency in beadmaking had been attained.

Materials used for beadmaking include gold, silver, copper; precious and semi-precious stones in great variety; bird, mammal, and fish bones, including teeth and ivory, and in some instances human bone; many kinds of marine and freshwater shells, and pearls, and finally vegetal materials. Seeds were easily strung and made into necklaces and other ornaments; specimens of such, in all probability prehistoric, have been found intact with their original strings in dry caves. Even modern Indians still have a fondness for seeds used in this manner. From the far Northwest there are examples of strung seeds of the silverberry (*Elæagnus argentea*), while in the tropics highly-colored seeds are greatly admired by the natives. As estheticism progressed among the ancient peoples they became more and more proficient in the manufacture of beads of a truly artistic character until ultimately remarkable results were achieved.

With the coming of Europeans to America there were introduced trade beads which were so highly prized by the natives that in many places they superseded the beads of native make. With noteworthy ingenuity the Indians developed an almost endless variety of objects calling for the use of trade beads, both for personal adornment and for the ornamentation of ceremonial and utilitarian articles.

The first record of the introduction of trade beads among the American Indians goes back to Columbus and his landing on Watling island on October 12, 1492.[1] His log states:

Soon after a large crowd of natives congregated there. . . . In order to win the friendship and affection of that people, and because I was convinced that their conversion to our Holy Faith would be better promoted through love than through force, I presented some of them with red caps and some strings of glass beads which they placed around their necks, and with other trifles of insignificant worth that delighted them and by which we have got a wonderful hold on their affections.

Oct. 15. A man from Conception Island was presented with a red cap and a string of small green glass beads.

This was the very beginning of the introduction and the use of foreign beads by the Indians. In later years travelers and traders found the natives on the mainland equally receptive, and from the

----

[1] From a translation of Las Casas's abridgment of Columbus's First Voyage, in Fox, G. V., An Attempt to Solve the Problem of the First Landing Place of Columbus in the New World, pp. 354–55, 360, Washington, 1882.

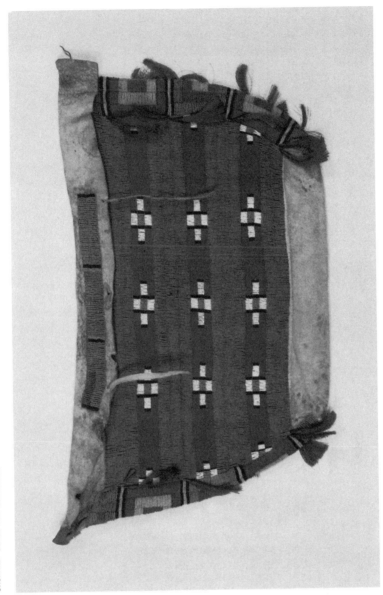

LARGE BAG FROM THE PONCA PEOPLE OF OKLAHOMA. (20/7645) 20½″ WIDE

(See back cover for color version.)

COTTON APRON, DECORATED WITH SEEDS, SHELLS AND BEADS. TOLOWA, CALIFORNIA.   (15/1703B) 21" x

(See inside front cover for color version.)

UMATILLA BEADED BAG, OREGON. (21/7902) 9″ x 10″

(See inside front cover for color version.)

ORCHARD—BEADS AND BEADWORK

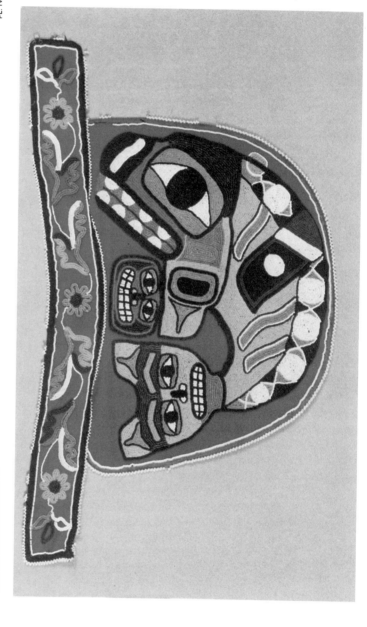

STROUDCLOTH BIB WITH KILLER WHALE DESIGN. TLINGIT, ALASKA.   (24/7455) 9½" x 15½"

(See front cover for color version.)

earliest historic times vast quantities of beads found their way among the Indians through various European channels, resulting in the well-known work in beads of glass and of other materials which has been so highly and artistically developed. That beads must have been an important factor in early trade is evident from the vast numbers that have been found in graves and on village-sites; and, judging by the great quantities of bead-embellished artifacts from many tribes and covering long periods down to the present time, there has been little diminution in the demand.

Prior to the use of beads as a form of embellishment, porcupine-quills dyed in varying colors were applied with unsurpassed workman-ship to garments and ornaments, producing exquisite designs.[2] The technique of quill decoration had attained such a high degree of per-fection at the time of the introduction of trade beads that the Indians found little or no difficulty in applying novel decorative methods with the new materials supplied them by Europeans.

The various techniques employed by the American Indians in pro-ducing their numerous forms of bead ornamentation, described in this memoir, are based on a study of the great number of specimens in the Museum of the American Indian, Heye Foundation. However extensive these collections may be, this account is not presented in the expectation that it will be found complete, for it is probable that other techniques may be shown by a study of other collections, while for the same reason other striking forms of beads of native make may have been omitted.

Various interesting references to the use of European beads in America are made by early travelers. Lewis and Clark,[3] for example, found a certain blue bead to have great value among the Indians of the Columbia River region, the bead referred to probably being the " cut-glass bead " found in great numbers in the Northwest. These explorers stated that

in the evening Seven indians of the *Clot sop*[4] Nation came over in a Canoe, they brought with them 2 Sea otter Skins for which they asked blue beads &c. and Such high prices that we were unable to purchase them without reducing our Small Stock of Merchendize, on which we depended for Subcistance on our return up this river. mearly to try the Indian who

---

[2] Orchard, W. C., The Technique of Porcupine-quill Decoration among the North American Indians, *Contr. Mus. Amer. Ind., Heye Found.,* vol. IV, no. 1, 1916. Reprinted 1971.

[3] Lewis and Clark, Original Journals, vol. III, p. 244, New York, 1905.

[4] The Clatsop, a Chinookan tribe on Columbia river, Oregon.

had one of those Skins, I offered him my Watch, handkerchief a bunch of red beads and a dollar of the American coin, all of which he refused and demanded ' *ti-â-co-mo-shack* ' which is *Chief beads* and the most common blue beads, but fiew of which we have at this time.

The writer wishes to acknowledge his great obligation to Dr. Elsie Fox, of New York City, for the X-ray photographs, reproduced herein, which have been so helpful in the study of bead drilling, and to Mr. Louis Rosenberg, the well-known bead manufacturer and importer, also of New York City, who has generously given his time and knowledge concerning trade beads.

W. C. Orchard

SHELL BEADS

F OR the manufacture of beads by the aborigines of America, no material was more commonly used than shell, as is shown by the vast numbers which from time to time have been recovered by excavation of ruins, village-sites, and graves throughout the two continents. Even since the introduction of glass beads there are individuals in some tribes of the United States and elsewhere who still practise the art of making beads of shell with primitive implements, the only adaptation of introduced tools being that of steel instead of stone for drill-points, and perhaps hammer and pincers. Many an Indian may still be seen in the Southwest wearing strings of beautifully made shell beads of recent manufacture, particularly among the Pueblo tribes. These are regarded as of far greater value than any beads of foreign introduction for the reason that shell is a sacred material which, coming from the water, in a measure symbolizes the power of that life-giving fluid to a people living in a semi-arid land whose religious practices have such an important relation to rainfall. It is only within comparatively recent years that glass beads have become popular with the Pueblos, and even now they are worn only by children to any considerable extent, although such beads found their way to these Indians with the coming of the first Spanish explorers and missionaries in the sixteenth century. A few objects of Pueblo manufacture, both ancient and modern, are decorated with glass beads, where flat surfaces could be covered. Sometimes Pueblo necklaces consist of beads, including those of shell, which the natives themselves have unearthed from ruins in their country.

The numerous forms of ancient shell beads have been so adequately described and illustrated in reports on archeological research that repetition will not be attempted. The chief forms of shell beads are discoidal, spherical, tubular, barrel-shape, ovate, rectangular, conical, truncate, and several odd forms in a wide range of sizes.

Many of the small marginella and olivella shells have been used with merely the point ground off or perhaps having an aperture made in the outer wall to permit the passage of a string. Dentalia likewise have been used as beads, with a string passing from end to end.

A large number of shell beads in a wide variety of sizes and shapes, usual with such material, were found by the Mrs. Thea Heye expedition to San Miguel island, California. Some of these are worthy of special mention by reason of their incised-line decoration. Fig. 1, *a,* is a truncated cone bearing cross-hatching around the sides and with a narrow plain band at the apex. In *b* is seen another form of truncated cone with panels of cross-hatching around the sides. In *c* and *d* are represented more or less spherical beads, the former having parallel lines encircling each end, with lengthwise lines between, the latter cross-hatched to within a slight distance of the perforation at each end. In *e* is

F I G. 1.—Shell beads from San Miguel island, California. Actual size. (9/5122, 9/5123, 9/5125).

shown one of a considerable number of small discoidal beads incised with cross-hatching over the circumference. The sizes of this group vary from about one-sixteenth to one-quarter of an inch in diameter, and are of proportionate thickness. Many of the smaller examples are made from the narrow ends of dentalium-shells.

The decoration applied to this series of beads is remarkable when their size is considered. We have no knowledge of the manner in which this minute engraving was done. It can only be surmised that a small sharp chip of stone, possibly mounted in a wooden handle with bitumen, formed the incising tool. To accentuate the ornamentation, the engraved lines were filled with black pigment, much of which still remains.

Beads made from the ends of dentalia show that the natural perforations were enlarged to accommodate a thread to fit them for use as necklaces or other ornaments. The drillings in the larger beads, which can be more easily seen, show the use of such primitive tools as would have been used before the introduction of steel by Europeans.

Fig. 2 illustrates one of about a hundred beads collected from the Santa Inés Indians of Santa Barbara county, California, made

F IG. 2.—Bead made from the hinge of a marine bivalve. Santa Inés Indians, Santa Barbara county, California. (6/3881).

from the hinge portions of a marine bivalve, probably the rock-oyster. All are more or less curved like that shown in the drawing, and each

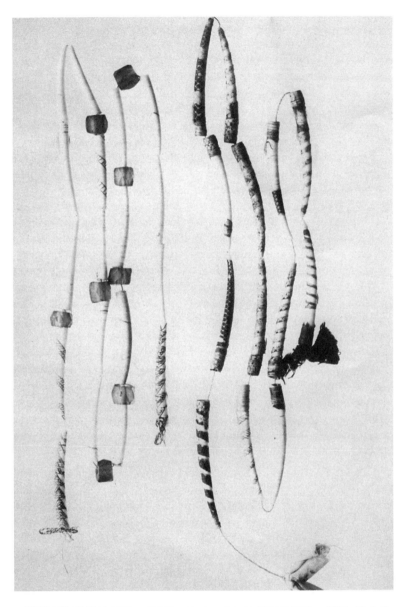

DENTALIUM SHELLS WITH INCISED AND SNAKE SKIN DECORATION.   HUPA OF CALI-
FORNIA.   (1/2537)

has a central depression. Perforations were made with a steel drill from each end, meeting in the center. In many cases the drilling reaches the surface in the depression, so that when the beads are strung the thread is there exposed. In several such beads the depression is filled with bitumen, and it is probable that all of them had once been similarly treated. The shell is white, veined with crimson, and in color presents a pleasing appearance; but uniformity of size being disregarded, the ensemble is rather disorderly.

Dentalium shells of the Pacific coast having been subjected to wide distribution through barter, they have been used as a medium of decoration by many tribes from the Pacific to the Atlantic. Some of the mid-continental tribes used them extensively, sewing them in patterns to their clothing and baby carriers, wearing them in the form of necklaces and in other ways. But besides being esteemed for their decorative value, among some of the California tribes dentalia became of even greater value as a medium of exchange. The shells vary in length from about an inch to nearly three inches; but only the long shells had a monetary value, that is, those exceeding about an inch and three-quarters, the value increasing with the length. The Hupa valuation of a large dentalium in early days was equivalent to five dollars, while the smallest represented fifty cents. A detailed description of the valuation is recorded by Goddard.[1] A source of information on the Shasta of northern California notes:

The property given for a wife formerly varied greatly, but an average price is said to have been one or two deerskins, fifteen or twenty long dentalia, ten or fifteen strings of disk beads, and twenty or thirty woodpecker-scalps.[2]

When used as money the shells were wrapped spirally with narrow strips of snake-skin, sometimes with fish-skin; or a short section of a small snake-skin, while soft and pliable, might be stretched on the shell. The large end was further embellished with a little tuft of red feathers from a woodpecker's crest.

Two strings of dentalium shell beads are shown in Pl. V. One has the regulation skin wrappings; the other, in all probability intended for a necklace, is interspersed with glass beads. Four of the shells are elaborately ornamented with incised lines into which black pigment has been rubbed to emphasize the etching.

---

[1] Goddard, P. E., Life and Culture of the Hupa, *Univ. Calif. Publ. Amer. Archaeol. Ethnol.*, vol. I, 1903.

[2] Dixon, R. B., The Shasta, *Bull. Amer. Mus. Nat. Hist.*, vol. XVII, pt. V, p. 465, 1907.

Several decorated dentalium shells bearing incised designs (fig. 3) were found at an archeological site in Washington. Possibly these shells were thus ornamented and used by California Indians, later finding their way to the north through intertribal barter and finally becoming prized possessions of their ultimate owners in Washington.

Two remarkable strings of beads were collected from the Santa Inés Indians of Santa Barbara county, California. These were made from sections of the smaller ends of dentalium shells, and are remarkable for their numbers. One string is eight and a half feet in length, the other forty-one and a half feet. Containing on an average of thirty-three beads to the inch, there are approximately twenty thousand beads in the two strings. Many of the beads are less than a sixteenth of an inch in diameter. Irregular ends, which would result when the sections were severed from the shell, have all been smoothly ground, and, perhaps owing to continued use, have received a high polish. Even if spread over a long period of time the manufacture of these two strings would have proved a task requiring prodigious patience.

F I G. 3.— Incised dentalium shell from Washington. (4/2956).

California has been a prolific source of small shell beads. Thousands of small discoidal beads made from the walls of olivella or marginella shells, an eighth of an inch, more or less, in diameter, have been found, in many cases retaining the slight curvature of the shell. No doubt many were made for purposes other than stringing as necklaces. Their uses are described in another section of this paper.

Other localities have yielded great numbers of similar beads, but not in such quantities as have been found in California.

Quantities of small shells of the genera marginella and olivella have been found from time to time during the exploration of mounds and graves, which have had their points ground off in order that a string might be passed lengthwise from point to lip and thus fit them for use as beads. In some instances they have been found in masses so disposed as to indicate their use as breast-ornaments or as decorations for robes, in which event broad surfaces had been covered. In other cases they have been found in such manner as to make obvious their use as necklaces. Again, they were scattered in such confusion that it was not possible to determine their purpose. Explorations by the Museum on Hiwassee island, Tennessee, brought to light several such cases.[3] Here Harrington reported finding two skeletons covered from chin to waist with olivella shells, which led to the belief that some kind of garment had been decorated with them. Another skeleton had the upper part covered with similar shells, which bore traces of having been worked into a pattern. Still another had a shell collar, while two had strings of shells which in all probability had served as necklaces. Disintegration had been so thorough in all these burials that the shells could not be removed and yet be kept in the relative positions in which they were found. The regular disposition was such that there is little or no doubt as to how the shells were used, although nothing re-

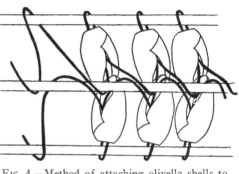

FIG. 4.—Method of attaching olivella shells to thongs. Modoc. (10/9600).

mained to indicate whether they had been sewn to a leather background or had been woven into a fabric.

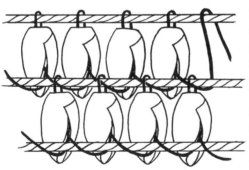

FIG. 5.—Method of attaching olivella shells to fiber cords. Modoc. (10/9601).

A leather robe collected in the latter part of the sixteenth or early seventeenth century, said to have been the "habit of Pohatan, King of Virginia," which is now in the Ashmolean Museum at Oxford, England, is ornamented with small seashells (*Marginella nivosa*) which have had their points ground off and have been sewn to the garment with threads of sinew. The design represents animal and human forms, and circular patterns (Pl. VI). There is every

[3] Harrington, M. R., Cherokee and Earlier Remains on Upper Tennessee River, *Indian Notes and Monographs, Museum of the American Indian, Heye Foundation*, misc. 24, 1922.

POWHATAN'S ROBE IN THE ASHMOLEAN MUSEUM, OXFORD

25

reason to believe that at least some of the material which Mr. Harrington found in Arkansas was originally of this form of decoration. Very little, if any, of this kind of work, aside from the

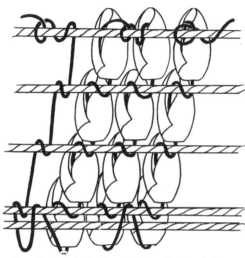

A s h m o l e a n garment, exists t o d a y . Several specimens of a woven technique made by modern Indians, however, are in the collections of the Museum of the American Indian, which may represent survivals of an old art. T h r e e specimens collected from the Modoc of California are in the form of neckornaments, each having a different method of attaching the shell beads, as shown in figs. 4–6. Fig. 4 illustrates the weaving on soft-tanned

FIG. 6.—Method of attaching olivella shells to fiber cords. Modoc. (10/9601).

leather thongs with fiber threads to fasten the shells, while the specimens represented in figs. 5 and 6 are supplied with a cord base and small threads to attach the shells to the cords. As the movements of the attaching threads are somewhat intricate, the drawings will indicate their trend more graphically than a description. Another ornament made of shells was collected from the Tigua Indians of Isleta pueblo, New Mexico (Pl. VII). In t h i s t h e cords a n d threads are made of a

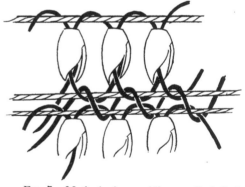

FIG. 7.—Method of assembling small shells in making a belt. Isleta, New Mexico. (5/240).

soft cotton material of native spinning. The movements of the

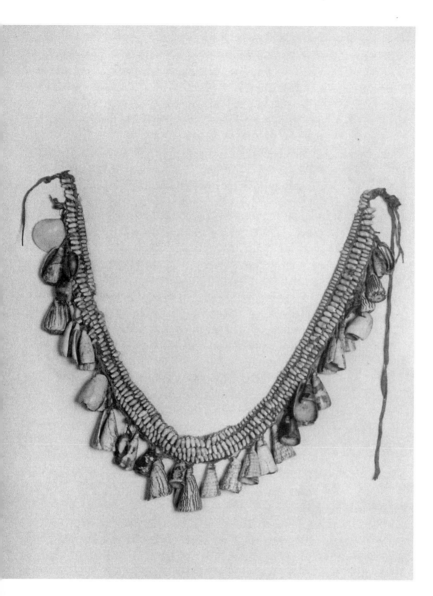

GIRDLE MADE OF SHELLS. ISLETA PUEBLO, NEW MEXICO. (5/240)

several threads are complicated, as is the case with the Modoc specimens, but are clearly shown in the drawing (fig. 7).

Lovelock cave, Nevada, has yielded specimens that reveal two interesting methods of attaching olivella-shells to strings for probable use as necklaces or bracelets.[3a]   Fig. 8 shows how two strings have

been used as a base, with a single string passed through a shell and knotted to the double string. A number of shells have been attached in this way with a knot between each two shells, all drawn tightly together so that the knots are covered by the lip of the shell. Fig. 9 illustrates the common crochet stitch in which the thread is made to loop through one loop after another. The shells are attached by passing the thread through from point to lip between loops. In this case the shells are not close together, but are separated by two or three loops. The threads are well made of some unidentified fiber.

It is evident from the quantities recovered that olivella shells were very popular wherever obtainable. They have been found in profusion in both the eastern and the western area of North America, and sparsely in the Middle West of the United States, where no doubt they found their way by intertribal barter.

FIG. 8.—Detail of tying of olivella-shells to a base composed of two strings. Nevada.   (13/4654).

FIG. 9.—Method of assembling shells in a crochet-like stitch. Nevada. (13/4653).

Other fragments were found in Lovelock cave with the shells strung on strips of leather and on fiber cords. The points of all the shells were ground off to permit the passage of a string. Two other interesting techniques were found in the same cave, consisting of

---

[3a] While this is passing through press the report on Lovelock Cave by L. L. Loud and M. R. Harrington (*Univ. Calif. Publ. Amer. Archæol. Ethnol.,* vol. 25, no. 1, Berkeley, 1929) makes its appearance. The authors describe (p. 105) three methods of attaching olivella shells, one of which is similar to that shown in our fig. 8, except that our specimen has but one knot between the shells. Further examination of a number of fragments in the Museum collections, however, discloses the two-knot variety.

some strung beads which were made from the outer wall of the olivella.

Fig. 10 illustrates a number of rectangular beads with grooved cuts across the convex side of the pieces of shell, instead of circular perforations. The grooves are cut deeply enough to penetrate the shell in the center of the curve. A strand of sinew was used to tie the beads, one overlapping the other, to a pair of fiber cords, a knot between each two beads. A pendant made from musselshell is at one end of the two strings.

The other technique is shown in eight fragments of what may have been a necklace. The combined length of the pieces is 21 inches, and there is every indication that they originally formed one piece. The beads are discoidal, three-sixteenths of an inch in diameter, with circular perforations. They are threaded on a fiber cord in such manner that one overlaps the other (fig. 11), and are held in place with a stitch similar to that shown in fig. 9.

Fig. 10.—Rectangular pieces of shell tied to fiber cords with sinew threads. Nevada. (13/4660).

Fig. 11.—Discoidal beads assembled with a crochet-like stitch. Nevada. (13/4647).

RUNTEES, OR SHELL DISCS

Shell ornaments of the kind known as *runtees,* believed to be an English corruption of the French *arrondi,* "rounded," have been found in widely separated localities in the East. They vary from an inch to an inch and three-quarters in diameter, and from an eighth to three-sixteenths of an inch or more in thickness. They are supplied with two lateral perforations. There has been some discussion as to the use of these objects, some authorities considering them more of the character of pendants than of beads. During the exploration of a Munsee cemetery in New Jersey a number of runtees were found in positon on two skeletons, clearly indicating their use as beads in necklaces.[4] On the other

---

[4] Heye, G. G., and Pepper, G. H., Exploration of a Munsee Cemetery near Montague, New Jersey, *Contr. Mus. Amer. Ind., Heye Found.,* vol. II, no. 1, 1915.

hand, in the Museum collections there is a Huron necklace consisting of wampum beads with a runtee so disposed on the string as to justify its designation as a pendant (Pl. VIII). Another Huron wampum necklace (Pl. IX) has a discoidal shell ornament, without the lateral perforations, which also is obviously a pendant. The terms bead and pendant, therefore, are arbitrary, and as it is not possible to segregate the two classes of objects either by size or by use, we shall treat the runtees as beads.

Seven runtees of approximately the same size were found with a burial in Cayuga county, New York,[5] ornamented with an incised design as shown in fig. 12, in which the parallel lines at the side indicate the thickness of the ornament and the position of the lateral perforations. Judging by the accuracy with which the conventional design on these runtees was produced, it is evident that they were made after the Indians had obtained iron implements, the pattern resulting from the use of a pair of dividers. The central point is very distinct on all the specimens, as are the points on the inner ring where the leg of the instrument was placed to incise the arcs that form the star-like design.

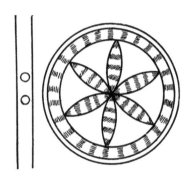

Fig. 12.—Diagram of a runtee from a grave in Cayuga county, New York. Actual size. (9/4831).

The cross-hatching between the lines made by the dividers was apparently scratched with a sharp-pointed implement. The perforation of each of these runtees is true and bears every indication of having been made with a steel drill, but how the implement was rotated we have no means of knowing. Nevertheless, the use of implements supplied by Europeans, rather than detracting from his artistic ability, enabled the Indian to conceive new if more conventional decorative patterns.

Reference will be made later to runtees of the Virginia Indians mentioned by Beverley.

Discoidal Beads

The most numerous of all shell beads are those of discoidal form, which in diameter range from a sixteenth of an inch to an inch and a half or more. Their distribution is wide; indeed they were made

---

[5] Skinner, Alanson, Notes on Iroquois Archeology, *Ind. Notes and Monogr., Mus. Amer. Ind., Heye Found.,* misc. 18, 1921, p. 63.

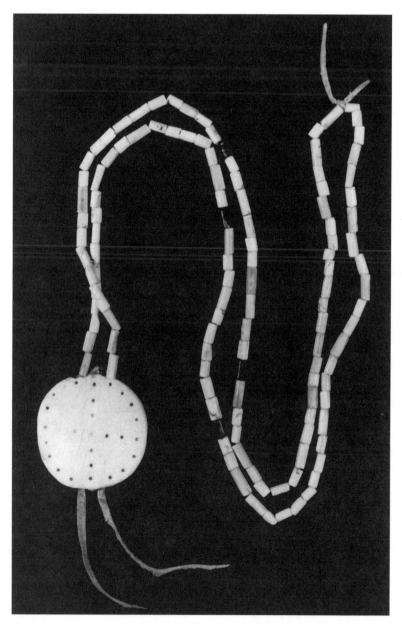

HURON NECKLACE OF WAMPUM BEADS WITH A RUNTEE ATTACHED. (11/7513)

wherever suitable shells were obtainable, and from the fact that sea-shells have been found far in the interior of the continent it is evident that the raw material and probably the finished articles passed from tribe to tribe through barter. On the Pacific coast, particularly among the tribes of California, such beads, from a quarter to a half of an inch in diameter, have been called wampum and were a medium of exchange; and similar beads were used for a like purpose by the Indians of the East.

The comparative ease with which discoidal beads could be made is perhaps the reason for their abundance. The method of manufacture has been observed at Zuñi pueblo, New Mexico, where they are still made in quantities. The principal implements are a pump-drill and a flat stone on which the shells are rubbed and shaped, although some of the more progressive beadmakers use also pincers for breaking the shells into suitable bits, somewhat larger than the finished bead is to be. Originally the shell was roughly shaped by means of a hammer-stone. In place of a stone drill-point, the end of a small three-cornered file is sharpened so that with a few revolutions of the pump-drill and the frequent application of water, the perforation of the roughly-shaped piece of shell is completed, first from one side, then from the other. The drilled pieces are then strung on a string eighteen inches or more in length, knotted at one end so that the un-finished beads may be crowded tightly on the string. A naked length of the string is held firmly in one hand and wrapped around with two or three turns. With the string of unfinished beads held in this manner a pressure exerted by the thumb on the last bead so crowds them together that they become almost rigid. In this condition the strung lengths are laid on the sandstone slab and rolled over the sur-face of the stone back and forth with the free hand, the hand holding the end of the string remaining stationary. Water and grit, some of which comes from the stone, are liberally supplied to facilitate the abrasion of the rough edges. A groove along one edge of the slab is provided as an adjunct to the smoothing operation. The beads are drawn back and forth in the groove, which helps to keep them of equal size. Sometimes a piece of wood with a corresponding groove is rubbed over the beads while lying in the stone groove.

By this process, not a very long one, a well-shaped and finished string of beads is produced. The shell most esteemed by the Zuñi for beadmaking is the *Olivella biplicata,* which has a slightly purplish tinge. Traders at Zuñi accept such beads in strings of about twenty-

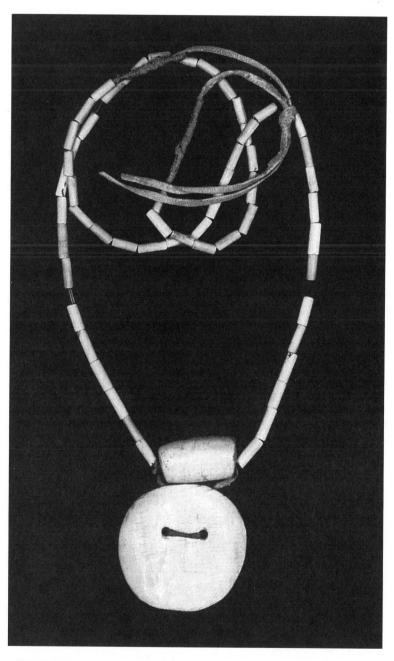

HURON NECKLACE OF WAMPUM BEADS WITH CIRCULAR SHELL PENDANT. (11/7514)

four inches in trade to the amount of two to three dollars, to the entire satisfaction of the Indians.

The same methods are applied by the Zuñi in their manufacture of turquois beads, but a much longer time is expended on these because of the hardness of turquois and the greater difficulty both of drilling and of grinding; besides, it is necessary to grind and polish both faces of a turquois bead, one bead at a time, a process not required in the case of the shell beads.

It may be assumed that most, if not all, of the prehistoric discoidal beads were made in the manner described, except, of course, that iron implements were not used.

Fig. 13 illustrates a shell bead or pendant of odd shape, one of a large number found in a grave in the vicinity of Taltal, Chile. All of them were perforated with a broadly tapering drill for stringing. They range in size from three-sixteenths to half an inch in width. There is nothing in connection with these objects to suggest how they were used. The protuberance at one end would prevent them from hanging regularly on a string in the form of a necklace, unless something of the character of tubular or disc beads were placed between them. Possibly they were assembled in a mass as a breast ornament, or sewn to a garment in some such manner as elk-teeth are used by some of the Indians.

Fig. 13.— Shell object used as a bead or pendant, from Taltal, Chile. (13/5141).

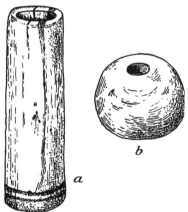

Fig. 14.—Massive shell beads from the Rio Ulua, Honduras. ¾. (4/3963).

Some massive shell beads (fig. 14) from the region of Ulua river, Honduras, are of two forms, tubular and globular, both rather crudely shaped, especially the spherical ones. The tubular beads are about three inches long by seven-eighths of an inch in diameter, and have unusually large perforations, as shown in the illustration. The perforations apparently were made by drilling from each end, and then smoothed throughout, so that the walls are nearly parallel. One end of several of the tubes is encircled with two incised lines, which, however, have suffered from disintegration of the shell.

The globular beads have smaller perforations, which likewise were made by drilling from each end in such manner as to taper toward the center, where the point of junction is more or less irregular in each case.

An odd type of shell object is illustrated in fig. 15. A number of this general form, both quadrilateral and

FIG. 15.— Ornament of shell from Santa Marta, Colombia. Actual size. (13/7701).

square, were obtained in Santa Marta, District of Magdalena, Colombia. In size they vary from a quarter to half an inch square, by seven-sixteenths to three-quarters of an inch long. There is a circular depression in each, made with a blunt-pointed reamer, through which are two perforations. A V-shape groove has been ground in each edge, probably for ornamentation. The fact that only one face has been thus treated suggests that these objects were not made to be strung in the usual manner, as in a necklace, while the two perforations would seem to indicate that they were designed to be sewn on a garment or on some ornament for personal adornment.

Another unusual shell form, represented in fig. 16, approaches an inverted U in shape, with a perforation through the center of the arc as indicated by the dotted lines. The mode of use of this object, as in the last specimen, is in doubt. It would of course be possible to string a number of such objects together, but their shape would suggest use as pendants rather than as beads.

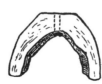

FIG. 17.— Notched rectangular shell bead from Santa Marta, Colombia. Actual size. (13/7702).

FIG. 16.—U-shape shell object from Santa Marta, Colombia. Actual size. (13/7703).

There were also obtained in Santa Marta a number of rectangular beads of shell (fig. 17), varying in size from five-sixteenths to five-eighths of an inch in length and one-eighth inch thick. They are deeply notched from two opposite edges toward the center and are provided with tapering perforations drilled from the narrow end of each notch. There is no evidence to justify the classification of these objects as beads. The lengthwise drilling would permit stringing, and it would also be possible to sew them to a flat surface of fabric or of tanned leather either as ornaments or as fastenings. These were found in association with the two odd forms from Santa Marta above described.

PEARL BEADS

Pearls from freshwater mussels have been perforated and used as beads. In the report on his researches on Tennessee river,[6] Mr. M. R. Harrington describes and illustrates several such beads; and Prof. F. W. Putnam, while excavating a mound near Madisonville, Ohio,[7] found "not less than fifty thousand pearls, most of them pierced and injured by heat." Ornaments made from haliotis pearls were found on San Miguel island, California,[8] during excavations by the Museum expedition. Some of them were undoubtedly used as beads.

BONE BEADS

The use of bone, especially bird-bone, for the manufacture of beads, was widespread, and with few exceptions the product is so nearly uniform in character and the method of manufacture, in all probability, so similar that a general description will include the entire class. Such beads have been found in abundance, particularly in Pueblo ruins of the Southwest,[9] where climatic and soil conditions are such that bone has been preserved for centuries.

The bones employed were usually the femur, ulna, or radius, preferably of birds, although corresponding bones from small mammals were also used.

Fig. 18 illustrates a series of unfinished and finished objects from the ruins of the Zuñi pueblo of Hawikuh which were probably intended for beads. Many bones were severed and ground for other purposes, and in some cases it is not possible to determine which were beads and which were not. The drawing shows a bone (a) which has been scored preparatory to breaking off two sections. The scoring or cutting was done with a sharp-edged flake of stone, or with a piece of thin sandstone which would cut in the manner of a file.

---

[6] Harrington, M. R., Cherokee and Earlier Remains on Upper Tennessee River, *Ind. Notes and Monogr., Mus. Amer. Ind., Heye Found.,* misc. 24, 1922.
[7] *Proc. Amer. Asso. Adv. Sci.,* 1884.
[8] Heye, G. G., Certain Aboriginal Artifacts from San Miguel Island, California, *Ind. Notes and Monogr., Mus. Amer. Ind., Heye Found.,* vol. VII, no. 4, 1921.
[9] Hodge, F. W., Hawikuh Bonework, *Ind. Notes and Monogr., Mus. Amer. Ind., Heye Found.,* vol. III, no. 3, 1920.

Another section of bone (*b*) indicates by the jagged edges that it was not cut off entirely by scoring, but was broken off when the cutting was carried far enough to insure easy breaking. So many such fragments have been found as to lead to the belief that this was the common procedure in the primary process of beadmaking from bone. In the finished bead or tube (*d*) the jagged edges have been smoothed, in all probability on a sandstone slab. This class of beads was no doubt very easy to produce, and it is found in a great variety of sizes.

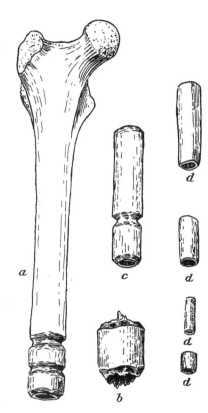

FIG. 18.—Unfinished and finished beads made of bone. Hawikuh, New Mexico.

Fig. 19 represents three beads collected from the Eskimo at Bristol bay and Point Hope, Alaska. They are of denser bone than those obtained from birds, and are skilfully made and ornamented with incised designs. The specimens shown in *a* has a number of circular depressions around the center, no doubt intended to hold inlays which may have been small glass beads. The ornamentation of objects with inlaid beads, a common practice among the Alaskan Eskimo, is elsewhere referred to in this paper (see page 162).

Two beads made from small bird-bones were found in a shellheap on Hog island near Pemaquid, Maine. One of them, although somewhat disintegrated, bears an incised design (fig. 20) typical of the art of the modern Indians of Maine and is found especially on thin wooden objects, such as knife-handles, splint-cutters, etc. Nothing of European origin was found in association with these two beads, but some stone skin-scrapers and a few fragmentary bone awls were in the same shellheap, while excavation nearby also revealed bone implements, as well as pottery fragments. The absence of European materials suggests that the beads were made before contact with whites, or at least before Caucasian influence had affected native arts by blending the ancient and modern decora-tive devices of these Maine Indians.

Sections of fish-vertebræ required little or no artificial perforation for stringing. They have been found in many parts of the country under conditions which point conclusively to their use as beads.

In addition to the use of bone for bead-making, teeth in their entirety have also been employed, especially in Central Amer-ica and South America, where small monkey-teeth, perforated laterally through the root ends, were strung in the form of necklaces and have a particularly striking appearance when graded according to size. The teeth

FIG. 19.—Bone beads from Alaska. *a, c,* Point Hope; *b,* Bristol bay. Actual size. (5/477; 9/123, 9/124).

of other animals have likewise been used by Indians in those parts both for necklaces and for other articles of adornment.

The Indians of northern North America used the teeth of buffalo, wolf, and elk. In modern times the teeth of domestic animals have not been scorned as objects for personal adornment.

FIG. 20.—Bone bead with incised decoration from Maine. Actual size. (9/3299).

The mandibles of certain crustaceans have been employed to a slight extent for making necklaces, but their shape does not lend itself to orderly arrangement as beads.

Perhaps the most gruesome of all neck-ornaments are human finger-tips that have been desiccated and perforated for stringing. Two such necklaces in the Museum, one from the Ute, were un-doubtedly prepared as charms rather than strictly for purposes of adornment. From such information as was obtainable it is learned that the finger-tips in one case were taken from a slain enemy, a state-ment not at variance with the recorded custom of taking a part of an especially valorous warrior in order that the victors might thus be-come embued with his spirit of bravery. Possibly the custom of tak-ing finger-tips bore some relation to that of extracting the heart of an enemy killed in battle and dividing it among the victors. Among Indians generally, however, such things were regarded with the same repugnance as by white people. Indeed there are some who have such great fear of the dead that they would not touch a corpse in any circumstance.

STONE BEADS

Fig. 21 illustrates a group of stone beads of the more common forms from Mexico. In several cases the beadmaker took advantage of the natural shape of a pebble and drilled it without any attempt at shaping. Very many such rude beads have been recovered during

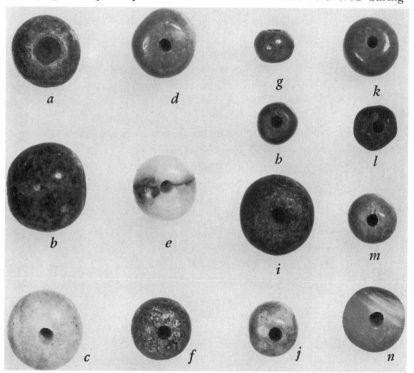

FIG. 21.—Various forms of stone beads from Mexico. Actual size.

excavations. It cannot be stated positively whether or not these were used for ornamental purposes; but it hardly seems probable that such were employed as objects of embellishment when we consider the remarkable degree of esthetic culture attained by the early Mexican tribes, unless, there having been a well-recognized caste system in ancient Mexico, the esthetic taste of the lower classes may have been satisfied with ornaments so crude. There is a possibility that these pebbles, unaltered except as to perforation, were used as tallies or counters, the fact that they are drilled not necessarily indicating that they were strung for use as necklaces. None of the Mexican fabrics reported by early chroniclers now survive, hence it is not possible to say that perhaps they were employed as loom-weights. Other beads. of this group are symmetrically shaped and polished, and no doubt were used for personal adornment. There is a variety of perforations—some are biconical, made with a blunt-pointed stone drill, others have nearly parallel borings effected with either a solid or a hollow drill of some material capable of carrying an abrasive. Fig. 21, *g, h, j,* are of jadeite; *i* is of Amazon stone; *k* is probably nephrite; the others are of unidentified stone.

In the Museum collections are many remarkable miniature stone beads from ancient Peru, Ecuador, New Mexico, Arizona, California, and Nevada. Most of these tiny beads are made of a black stone, some identified as steatite. From Hawikuh, New Mexico,[10] there are a number of beads of turquois, and thousands fashioned from the same material were found in the ruins of Pueblo Bonito [11] in Chaco cañon of the same state, among which are some very diminutive ones. Most of these turquois beads are discoidal. Some have tapering perforations, others apparently were drilled through uniformly. It is probable that the tapering apertures in some of the softer stone were afterward worked straight in the process of finishing the beads, while those of other beads were worn evenly from long use on a string. Turquois beads and other ornaments have been found in many localities south of the Pueblo region through Central America to the Argentine Republic.

FIG. 22.—Enlarged drawing representing the form of miniature stone beads and the two kinds of drilling. The central dot illustrates the actual size of some of these beads. Peru.

Fig. 22 illustrates the shape of the miniature beads and the two kinds of perforations. The size of the beads varies from about one-sixteenth of an inch and less in diameter, and are proportionately thin. Some of the perforations are so small that it seems almost incredible that a stone-pointed drill could have been used, yet that is

[10] Hodge, F. W., Turquois Work of Hawikuh, New Mexico, *Leaflet no. 2, Mus. Amer. Ind., Heye Found.,* 1921.

[11] Pepper, G. H., Pueblo Bonito, *Anthr. Papers Amer. Mus. Nat. Hist.,* vol. xxvii, New York, 1920.

the only plausible way in which such work could have been accomplished. After the introduction of iron by Europeans the operation would have been comparatively simple. Many of these beads, however, were found under such conditions as to leave no doubt of their prehistoric origin.

The method employed by modern Indians in manufacturing discoidal stone beads is the same as that described for shell beads of similar form: that is, to shape the stone roughly with the white man's tools, such as hammer, pincers, and file. The pieces are next bored with a steel point rotated with a pump-drill or perhaps with a bow-drill (figs. 45, 46). The drilled pieces are then strung on a wire or a string, and the edges are ground and smoothed on a flat or a grooved stone provided with fine grit and water, until discs

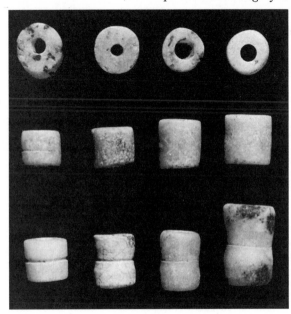

Fig. 23.—Calcite beads from Jamaica. Actual size. (12/575–578).

as nearly perfect as possible are produced. The faces of the disc are also smoothed by rubbing on a flat stone. The prehistoric peoples undoubtedly employed similar methods, using chipping implements made of bone or antler, and hammerstones, instead of metal tools. What motive power was employed for their drills is not positively known; but the spindle-whorl was in use in prehistoric times, and there is every reason to believe that the same principle was applied to a drill. The tiny bead represented with the enlarged drawings in fig. 22 is one which, with others, came from Peru.

Fig. 23 illustrates a series of calcite beads from Jamaica. They have biconical perforations, apparently made with a stone-pointed drill. Some of the beads are constricted and incised at the middle, and supplied with a lateral perforation at that point.

Fig. 24 illustrates a stone bead approaching the shape of a pear, unique both in form and decoration, found in Mississippi. The parallel perforation is through the center from top to bottom. The surface is incised and inlaid with fine threads of silver, which apparently have been rubbed or burnished with some such object as a polishing stone, causing the metal to spread and grip the rough edges of the incisions, thus holding it in place. The design suggests leaf-stems or grasses.

Fig. 24.—Stone bead inlaid with silver, from Mississippi. Actual size. (7601).

Represented in the Museum collections from Mexico, Central America, Colombia, and Ecuador, are beads of rock-crystal in various forms and sizes. Fig. 25 illustrates an example from the Valley of Mexico, oblate spheroid in form, three-quarters of an inch in maximum diameter and seven-sixteenths of an inch following the perforation. The conical perforation was drilled from each end, meeting at the center in a small opening. A broad-pointed stone drill may have been used to commence the drilling, but by reason of the high polish of the wall of the perforation it is reasonably certain that some such implement as a wooden rod was used with some fine abrasive material to complete the work. The surface of the bead is similarly polished.

Fig. 25.—Bead of rock-crystal from the Valley of Mexico. Actual size. (5/6977).

Outline drawings of tubular beads of rock-crystal from Santa Marta, Colombia, are presented in fig. 26. These are of interest because of the drillings, which may be clearly seen in the specimens and are indicated by dotted lines in the drawings. The complete bead shown in *a* is bored from each end toward the center, the tapering aperture bearing evidence of the wearing of the drill as the operation progressed. In this instance a stick was probably used as a drill, which was capable of carrying a fine grit during its revolutions: an arduous task indeed when one considers the hard material of which the beads are made. Nothing is known of the method of revolving the drill in this example. There are several ways in which the operation may have been performed: these are described in another section of this paper. The dotted lines show, by the perforations not meeting at the center, that the drill was not held true, which is frequently the case when perforations were made from each end of a bead of this type.

Fig. 26, *b,* shows a fragment of a bead, one end of which is polished, while the other is fractured. The drilling in this instance was

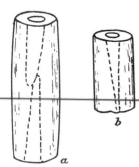

evidently made with a shaft of wood which wore away more rapidly than that used for drilling the other specimen. Both are beautifully polished on the outer surface. From the same place there are several other beads of this class, of sizes ranging from a quarter of an inch to two inches long, all of them equally well finished.

FIG. 26.—Crystal beads from Santa Marta, Colombia, showing drilling. ¾. (13/7715, 7716).

In the same collection are forty or more small discoidal beads of rock-crystal, from three-sixteenths to three-eighths of an inch in diameter and from one-sixteenth to three-sixteenths of an inch thick. These were all perforated from both sides with an extremely wide-angle drill-point, the tapering depressions averaging half the width of the bead.

From the same place in Colombia are a number of cylindrical beads of carnelian, ranging in length from three-eighths of an inch to three

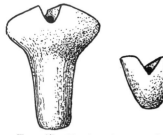

FIG. 27.—Beads of unusual shape from Magdalena, Colombia. Actual size. (13/7723, 7724).

FIG. 28.—Stone bead from Santa Marta, Colombia. Actual size. (7/7717).

inches. All are remarkably well fashioned and polished. Their perforations were made by the method employed in drilling the crystal beads.

In this group are included some odd-shaped objects, also made of carnelian, which from their drilling were evidently intended to be used as beads. The forms are illustrated in fig. 27. Each is notched at one end; the perforations are lengthwise, one extremity being at the bottom of the notch.

Discoidal, barrel-shape, and spherical beads, from one-quarter to about seven-eighths of an inch in diameter, are represented in the carnelian group. All of them were made with the same care and skill as the beads of rock-crystal, and evidently are the product of the same people.

Another unusual form of beads, from the same region in Colombia, is shown in fig. 28. There are several of this kind from three-sixteenths to seven-sixteenths of an inch in length. The perforation is shown by the dotted line. These objects are of a hard gray stone, and although properly classifiable as beads, they may have been used more as pendants. The knotted end of a cord might easily be concealed in the tapering perforation.

Worthy of mention are six four-sided tubular beads of catlinite from Ledyard, Cayuga county, New York, five-eighths of an inch to two and a quarter inches in length, by an eighth to three-sixteenths of an inch in breadth. All of them have been perforated from end to end with a steel drill. Except for the drilling they are not examples of fine workmanship, as the sides are misshapen.

Beads of many kinds of stone have been found throughout the continent, but so far as the Museum collections are concerned, Mexico has contributed a far greater number than any other area. Most of these are of simple forms, such as are shown in fig. 21, drilled for suspension without other artificial modification. Other forms are tubular, cubical, barrel-shape, and spheroidal. In addition to artificial shaping, some examples are decorated. A few are fashioned in the form of a muskmelon, with deeply cut and rounded ribs; others, of the tubular type, are embellished with incised lines around the ends. All are beautifully shaped and polished.

Beads similar to those of Mexico have been found in Central America as well, but they are not so numerous. California [12] has yielded large numbers of stone beads of many sizes. The simple ones are of hard stone, but when it was desired to produce more or less elaborate

[12] Heye, G. G., Certain Aboriginal Artifacts from San Miguel Island, California, *Ind. Notes and Monogr., Mus. Amer. Ind., Heye Found.,* vol. VII, no. 4, 1921.

beads the readily worked steatite was used. In fig. 28A is shown a representative series of beads from San Miguel island.

From California also are beads of amethyst, but these are relatively few, perhaps because of the scarcity of the material or the difficulty of working it.

Fig. 28A.—Steatite beads from San Miguel island, California. Actual size. (9/5018, 9/5019, 9/5021-25).

Among the objects from Peru is a tubular bead of lapis lazuli, beautifully shaped and polished, about three-quarters of an inch long and a quarter of an inch in diameter.

DRILLING

Vast numbers of beads fashioned by the natives from stone, shell, bone, and metals have been recovered during the excavation of both prehistoric and historic sites. In style they vary from the extremely rude to the most elaborate and ornate in form and design; indeed it would be difficult to praise too highly the skill displayed in the manufacture of some of the beads of the ancient Americans. So remarkable are the perforations of some of the beads of bone, shell, and particularly stone, that the student is puzzled to know how they were made. Metal beads, later to be described, were so fashioned that drilling was unnecessary. Bone offers little resistance to a stone-pointed drill, or even to a drill made entirely of wood when used with grit as a cutting agent, and shell may be drilled by the same process with almost equal ease.

The method of perforating thin discoidal beads of bone or shell is simple. A hard stone point set in the end of a wooden shaft and revolved in alternating directions between the hands quickly penetrated these materials; but if the object to be drilled was very hard

Fig. 29.—X-ray photograph of shell beads from Niagara county, New York, showing drilling. (8/8550). Photograph by Dr. Elsie Fox.

stone, more time would necessarily have been required. If drilled from one side only, a tapering perforation resulted. The drilling of globular or tubular beads was usually commenced from opposite sides. In cases where a stone drill-point was used, the perforation became more or less biconical according to the shape of the point; but if another type of point was used, such as a rod of wood or a reed with sand as an abrasive, the wall of the perforation had a tendency to be uniform. So far the drilling is a comparatively easy process, if time and patience are not considered; but when some of the long, slender, tubular beads are examined,—examples that show it to have been far from probable that a stone-pointed drill was used,—one gains no positive knowledge of the manner in which the perforations were made. Many kinds of drills of various materials have been suggested as having been used for this purpose.[13] It is well known that sand used in conjunction with a rod of wood of suitable texture will cut the hardest stone, hence one may conjecture that some such materials were employed in boring the long tubular beads referred to. For such a drill the wood must of course be just tough enough to hold the grains of sand firmly in its surface. Soft wood could not thus hold the sand and it would wear away much more quickly than the

[13] Handbook of American Indians, *Bull. 30 Bur. Amer. Ethn.*, pt. 1, Washington, 1907, *s.v.* Drills and Drilling. McGuire, J. D., A Study of the Primitive Methods of Drilling, *Rep. U. S. Nat. Mus. for 1894*, Washington, 1896. Holmes, W. H., Handbook of Aboriginal American Antiquities, *Bull. 60 Bur. Amer. Ethn.*, pt. 1, Washington, 1919.

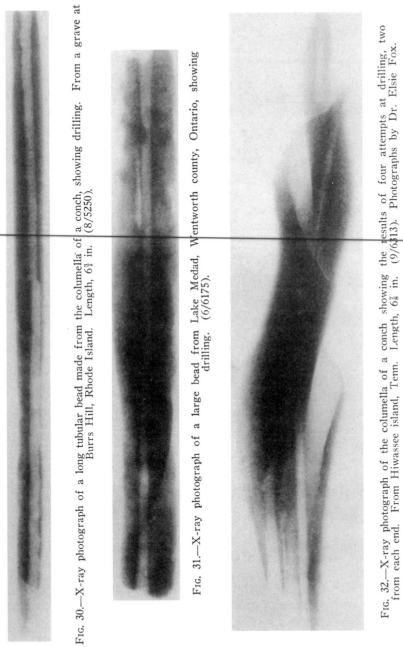

Fig. 30.—X-ray photograph of a long tubular bead made from the columella of a conch, showing drilling. From a grave at Burrs Hill, Rhode Island. Length, 6¾ in. (8/5250).

Fig. 31.—X-ray photograph of a large bead from Lake Medad, Wentworth county, Ontario, showing drilling. (6/6175).

Fig. 32.—X-ray photograph of the columella of a conch showing the results of four attempts at drilling, two from each end. From Hiwassee island, Tenn. Length, 6⅞ in. (9/6313). Photographs by Dr. Elsie Fox.

material being perforated, as would likewise be the case with wood that was too hard to allow the sand to become embedded.

FIG. 33.—X-ray photograph of a long tapering cylindrical bead made from the columella of a conch, showing drilling. The cross lines are the convolutions of the shell. From Santa Barbara, California. (2/3370). Photograph by Dr. Elsie Fox.

Reproductions of a number of X-ray photographs by Dr. Elsie Fox are introduced (figs. 29–37) to illustrate some of the remarkable results obtained by drilling. Some of the objects may appear to be

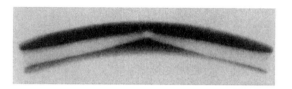

FIG. 34.—X-ray photograph of a bead made from haliotis-shell, from Santa Cruz island, California, showing drilling. (6/3157). Photograph by Dr. Elsie Fox.

too long for use as beads; but from the nature of their finish, the amount of work evidently expended on them, and the fact that they are drilled from end to end for the accommodation of a string or a

FIG. 35.—X-ray photograph of a stone bead from St. Davids, Ontario, showing drilling. (5/4169). Photograph by Dr. Elsie Fox.

thong, they may perhaps be so classed. It may be mentioned that most of the objects illustrated were made before the introduction of metal tools.

Judging from the borings of the tubes, the most feasible method by which the work could have been accomplished was by the use of a

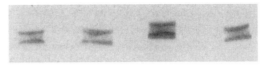

FIG. 37.—X-ray photograph of four cylindrical beads of turquois from Pueblo Bonito, New Mexico, showing drilling. Actual size. (5/1162). Photograph by Dr. Elsie Fox.

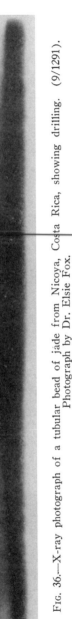

FIG. 36.—X-ray photograph of a tubular bead of jade from Nicoya, Costa Rica, showing drilling. (9/1291). Photograph by Dr. Elsie Fox.

rod and sand. Several methods of rotating the drill may have been known to the makers, other than the tedious processes of twirling it between the hands or of rolling it along the thigh with one hand while holding the object being perforated against the point of the drill with the other.

A good example of drilling is shown in fig. 38, which illustrates a broken shell bead from Lake Valencia, Venezuela. The boring has been done from each end, apparently with a solid drill, probably of wood, with grit as a cutting agent. The markings on the wall of the perforation clearly show where particles of the grit, adhering to the drill during a number of revolutions, have cut deeply into the shell. The tapering perforation is the result of the wearing of the drill as the operation proceeded. The lower part of the fracture shows the meeting point of the drilling from the two ends.

An odd feature is presented in the drilling of many stone beads from some of the islands of the West Indies. These beads are all tubular, and some bear incised decoration. In addition to the usual lengthwise perforation, a lateral drilling has been made. Fig 39 illustrates a bead treated in this manner, collected with others in Santo Domingo. The dotted lines indicate the courses of the two perforations. Nothing in connection with these beads has been found that would suggest the purpose of the extra perforation. Similar specimens have been found in Montserrat, St. Vincent, Jamaica, Cuba, and Porto Rico.

A number of tubular stone beads with unusual perforations have been found in Guerrero, Mexico. They range from three-quarters of an inch to about two inches in length, and are of the same general form as that shown in fig. 40, *a*, which is of nephrite and measures an inch and a quarter in length. Instead of the perforation passing entirely through the bead, short drillings have been made from each end, which are met by others bored in the sides.

A discoidal jade bead from Guerrero (fig. 40. *b*) has been partly drilled with a hollow drill. The core is intact, with the exception of a small flake broken from the top. For some reason this drilling was not finished, but a smaller perforation was made through the core. The implement used for the larger drilling was hollow, with sand as an abrasive; but as its wall is slightly undercut from the top down, the use of a metal cylinder that had spread during the drilling is suggested, rather

FIG. 38.—Fragment of a shell bead from Lake Valencia, Venezuela, showing drilling. Actual size. (6/1641).

than a reed, which would have worn quickly and made a boring that would have become smaller in diameter as it proceeded. The smaller perforation, which tapers very slightly, in all probability was made with a solid pointed drill of wood or bone, or of some such material capable of carrying a sharp cutting grit as the drill revolved. Hollow

FIG. 39.— Stone bead from Santo Domingo, W. I., with two perforations. Actual size. (13/6190).

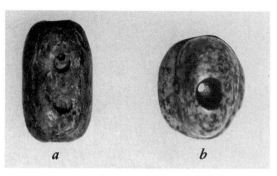

a   *b*

FIG. 40.—Stone beads from Guerrero, Mexico. Actual size. (9/3118, 1/1202).

metal drills have been described by McGuire.[14] Fig. 41 ilustrates a drill with the cutting edge made of sheet-copper wrapped around a wooden rod which constitutes the drill-shaft. The fact that the edges of the copper are not soldered or fused makes it possible for such a drill-point to expand during its revolutions. There is no positive information as to the method of revolving the drills, but some reproductions of two native Mexican drawings (figs. 42, 43) show

FIG. 41.— Tubular drill.

FIG. 42.—Hand-drill. From a Mexican painting in the Bodleian Library, Oxford. (*After McGuire*)

drills revolved between the palms of the hands of the workmen. A typical stone point for a drill is illustrated in fig. 44, showing a method of lashing the point in the split end of a wooden shaft.

FIG. 43.—Rotating the hand-drill. From a Mexican painting in Oxford University. (*After McGuire*)

[14] A Study of the Primitive Methods of Drilling, *Rep. U. S. Nat. Mus. for 1894*, Washington, 1896.

The bow drill, the pump drill, and probably the strap drill were
known from early times, and there is every reason for attributing at
least some of the bead perforations to the use of one or the other of
these effective implements.   The long tubular bead from Costa Rica

(fig. 36) exhibits an expenditure of many days'
labor in the drilling alone, without considering
the amount of work necessary to smooth and
polish the exterior.

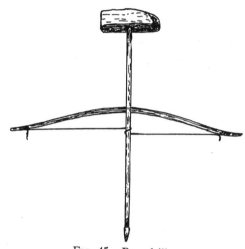

FIG. 44.—Typ-
ical   drill-point
of stone, show-
ing m o d e of
lashing.

FIG. 45.—Bow drill.

Fig. 45 represents the usual form of bow drill.   The shaft is shown
with a block on its upper end; this may be of wood or of any other
suitable material, and is furnished with a depression in which the
shaft revolves.   The purpose of the block is to hold the shaft in its
required position while the perforation is being made, and to exert
the proper amount of pressure or weight.   Many of the Eskimo
make the block so that it may be conveniently held between the teeth,
and it is supplied with a stone or an ivory socket to receive the shaft,
thus giving the worker a free hand for holding the object to be drilled.
In other parts of the continent the block is held in one hand while the
bow is worked with the other; in this case an assistant is required to
hold the object, unless some other means has been contrived.

The pump drill (fig. 46), a very efficient implement, consists of a
vertical shaft, a disc or spindle-whorl, and a horizontal cross-bar provided with a round aperture large enough to slide freely up and down

the shaft. A string is attached to each end of the cross-bar and passed through a small hole at the upper end of the shaft, or otherwise is secured at that point. Several twists of the shaft wrap the string around spirally and at the same time draw the cross-bar toward the top of the shaft. Downward pressure on the cross-bar unwraps the string and revolves the shaft, which, by the added momentum g i v e n by the disc acting as a fly-wheel, wraps the string around the shaft again in the opposite direction and draws up the cross-bar ready for another downward pressure. These movements keep the drill revolving first in one direction, then the other. The pressure is controlled mainly by the weight of the disc, which may be made of wood, stone, or pottery, attached firmly to the shaft. Any kind of cutting point may be secured in the end of the shaft. Two forms are shown in figs. 41 and 44—one a tubular drill of thin copper, the other a stone point lashed to the shaft.

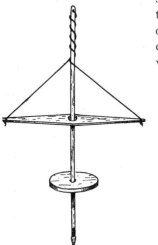

FIG. 46.—Pump drill.

FIG. 47.— Agate bead from Cana- zas, Prov- ince of Vera- guas, Pana- ma. ¾. (13/ 1837).

From a number of agate beads found at Canazas, Province of Veraguas, Panama, one is selected to show the manner of drilling. Fig. 47 illustrates the form, the dotted lines indicating the course of

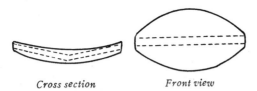

Cross section   Front view

FIG. 48.—Ovoid bead of shell from San Luis Obispo county, California, showing drilling. ½. (11/3948).

the perforation which has been made from each end of the bead. The beads belonging to this group are not all of the same form and size, some being tubular and others spherical or nearly so. But they all bear the same remarkably fine polish, to produce which, even with modern implements such as are used by a lapidary, would be no slight undertaking. The labor expended by primitive workers, therefore, in making such a bead with a stone hammer perhaps to shape the object roughly, other stone implements to smooth and polish the surface, and hardwood splints and sand to make the perforations, can perhaps be imagined. Beads of agate have been found wherever the material is native.

Fig. 48 represents a shell bead made from the wall of a conch, from San Luis Obispo county, California. The curvature of the shell would not permit a straight perforation from one end, hence, as the drawing indicates, the drilling was made from each end, meeting in the center. The appearance of this perforation would suggest the use of a wooden drill with sand.

METAL BEADS

BEADS OF GOLD

Perhaps the most remarkable of all beads made by early Americans are some of those fashioned from gold. Many have been brought together for the Museum from various localities in Central America and South America. A very large number of such beads came to light at La Tolita on the Island of Tola near the mouth of Santiago river, north of the city of Esmeraldas, Ecuador. Negroes living in the vicinity of La Tolita have from time to time dug in the mud for gold. These operations have yielded quantities of beads and other ornaments of such exquisite design and workmanship as to be worthy of the highest praise for their minute detail of execution. Indeed some of the work is so microscopic that it is difficult to understand how some of the objects could have been made without the aid of a magnifying glass and the delicate tools of a modern jeweler. According to Prof. M. H. Saville these objects are all examples of pre-Columbian art.

The beads alone will be described in this paper; the other ornaments will be the subject of another publication. With these finished objects quantities of prepared gold and unfinished specimens were found, but practically nothing that sheds light respecting the character of the tools used in their manufacture, with the exception of about a dozen small chisel-like objects of gold which indeed may be no more than prepared material, and some pieces of thin beaten gold in the form of tweezers.

Under the classification of prepared gold there are some small pellets, ranging from about one sixty-fourth of an inch to about one-eighth of an inch in diameter, many of which have been used in the manufacture of beads and other ornaments. It has been suggested that these pellets may have been made in some such way as bird-shot was formerly manufactured, i.e., by pouring melted metal through a screen and allowing it to fall from a greater or lesser height into water. Dr. E. P. Robinson, of Newport, Rhode Island, who is greatly interested in mechanics of ancient peoples, has demonstrated a method of producing small pellets of gold in a manner much more practicable, and has probably employed the same method as did the goldworkers of La Tolita. With the aid of a blowpipe and a flame Dr. Robinson has reduced some small pieces of gold to a molten state on an asbestos block. As soon as they reached that state they assumed a globular form which they retained after cooling.

There is little doubt that the ancient Indian goldsmiths understood the value of a blowpipe and used it, but of what it was made we can only surmise. A hollow reed would answer the purpose, and as nothing of a less perishable material has so far been found, we may assume that something of the kind was employed.

FIG. 49.—Enlarged photograph of a bead made of gold pellets fused together. The small object in the corner shows the actual size of the bead. Ecuador. (1/7452).

Other forms of prepared material from La Tolita are in the shape of wires of various gauges, and strips or ribbons that appear to have been beaten into shape rather than drawn. There are also some sheets of gold which no doubt were hammered into shape. It is not improbable that an assortment of tools, probably of stone, were overlooked by the treasure-hunters in their zealous search for the precious metal.

In some cases the beads and other ornaments have been made of a combination of the forms of prepared material, and in others entirely of one form, but in every instance remarkable perfection of workmanship is shown.

Fig. 49 illustrates a bead made entirely of globules or pellets composed of six rows or tiers with six globules in a row. There is an opening through the middle of the group for the passage of a string. The illustration reproduces an enlarged photograph of the specimen and also of the bead in its actual size, three-sixteenths of an inch long. There are many specimens of beads fashioned in this manner which are smaller in their ensemble and are composed of smaller globules; but the larger specimen was selected for convenience in illustrating. In this type of bead, globules of uniform size were placed together in tiers, probably around a central core of non-fusible clay or mud to hold them in place while being permanently brought into an insepa-rable mass, apparently by fusing. Many specimens have been ex-amined with a view of substantiating the theory that fusing was em-ployed, but no trace of anything suggesting the use of solder has been discovered. On the other hand there are a number of specimens showing where the parts have run together, their identity being al-most lost, in all probability owing to the application of too great heat. The spaces between the globules illustrated in fig. 49 show distinctly where the gold was melted just enough to form a bridge between the component parts, some of the joints showing a greater amount of fusion than others. Some form of flux must have been used to bring about the proper union of the globules, but what it was is, like the tools, an unanswered question. After the fusion had taken place, the core, if of the material suggested, could easily be removed, leaving the clear perfor-ation found in all the beads of this kind.

Fig. 50 illustrates a circlet composed of twelve globules fused to a hoop of wire. This particular form may have been made for some purpose other than a bead. It is of interest, however, on account of the size and regularity with which the globules are disposed around the ring.

Fig. 50.—Enlarged pho-tograph of a gold circlet with pellets attached. The actual size of the specimen is shown in the corner. Ecuador. (1/1229).

The objects shown in fig. 51 without doubt were made for use as beads. The globules are mounted between two rings of wire fused together. In *b* of this figure is shown an imperfect ring on the upper side; the ends are not cut square and have not been brought together, but few cases of this kind occur.

Fig. 52 presents an intricate twisting of a wire around the globules between the rings above and below. Considering the actual size of the bead, which is shown by the side of the enlargement, it is difficult to reach a conclusion as to how the parts were held together, let alone being shaped, before fusing.

In fig. 53 are shown the large central beads forming part of the necklace illustrated in fig. 61. The larger one is composed of twelve globules mounted between two hoops of twisted square wire, and the whole between hoops of round wire, four rings in all. The maximum diameter of this example is a quarter of an inch.

Fig. 54 illustrates a more complicated piece of work, consisting of twelve glob-

Fig. 51.—Enlarged photographs showing the fusion of gold pellets and rings. The actual size of the objects is shown in the corners. Ecuador. (1/7453).

Fig. 52.—Enlarged photograph of a bead composed of gold pellets and entwining wire. Ecuador. Note the actual size shown in the corner. (1/7453).

ules with a square wire interwoven. In the figure two of the rows of globules are obscured, but the ornament presents the same appearance on the opposite side. The passage for a string is lengthwise of the bead, and the square wire is looped at each end, making circular openings. The actual size of the bead is shown by the side of the enlargement.

The enlarged photograph of a tubular bead reproduced in fig. 55 commands special interest for the reason that this ornament is not composed of the usual globules and wire, but is formed from a piece of thin sheet-gold, with a pattern, evidently produced by hammering or by pressure, representing a series of wires turning spirally around the tube and encircling the openings at each end, while between the wires a number of globules are inserted. An overlapping joint extends lengthwise of the bead where the pattern matches perfectly, displaying remarkable skill in workmanship. The overlapping joint has the appearance of having been fused rather than soldered.

FIG. 53.—Enlarged photograph of two beads made of gold pellets and wire. Ecuador. Actual size of the beads is shown in the corner. (1/1229).

FIG. 54.—Enlarged and actual size of a gold bead composed of pellets and wire. Ecuador. (1/7456).

In fig. 56 is shown a group of small rings of varying diameters, each composed of a number of gold globules fused together, which may be incomplete parts of beads to which hoops of wire were to have been added, or they may have been made for use as ornaments other than beads.

Fig. 57, a, b, reproduce photographs enlarged and in actual size of a form which is very suggestive of beads. Quantities are in the collection, and are of varying sizes. This particular form does not occur as parts of other ornaments from La Tolita, and as there are many of them which are of uniform size as to length and diameter of wire, there is justification for classing them as beads. With very few exceptions they are made of a rounded wire wrapped spirally, probably around a core of the desired size, which could be withdrawn when the wrapping was completed. This core may have been another piece of gold wire. The exceptions are some that are made of a wire which has the appearance of having been rolled from a square strip, probably between two flat stones. Lengthwise irregularities visible on the rounded surface are shown distinctly in the enlargement (fig. 57, *c*), which indicate where the edges of the square strips may have been turned over in the rolling operation, causing the irregularities to appear. Such markings might occur on a drawn wire, but it is hardly possible that the early goldworkers knew anything of that process of wire-making.

A group of spheroidal beads made of thin sheet-gold is shown in fig. 58. They are composed of two hemispherical parts. The sheet-gold must have been pressed or hammered into a die made of some

material much harder than the gold, which would resist the pressure and allow the gold to be shaped into a small cup-like form. It is possible the die may have been made of stone, as might have been a stamp to fit the die, for many of the beads are of the same shape and size. The edges of the cup-like sections have been brought together, some overlapping a little, and the two parts fused into one. It is possible that the joint was rubbed or smoothed, since many of the finished

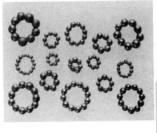

FIG. 55.—Enlarged photograph of a bead of sheet-gold made to represent the pellet-and-wire technique. Ecuador. The actual size of the bead is shown at the side. (1/7456).

FIG. 56.—Rings formed of pellets of gold. Ecuador. (1/7426).

beads show little if any joint, hence their appearance of having been made after the cup-like pieces were formed, but before they were fused together. A few of the spheroidal beads are provided with a collar of wire around the perforations (fig. 59).

A series of hollow beads, illustrated in fig. 60, are ornamented with pressed designs. Although very much battered, three in this group show conclusively that they were made in the same die, in two pieces and in the manner described for the beads shown in fig. 58. These designs alone establish the fact that a form of stamp and die was used by the ancient artisans in the manufacture of h o l l o w beads.

Fig. 61 portrays a necklace of beads made of globules between two or more rings which are shown in detail in fig. 53. It is not intended to convey the impression that the beads are on the original string. The conditions at La Tolita are such that anything of such a perishable nature as a string, whatsoever the material, would have disappeared through decay.

Other parts of South America, and also Central America, have yielded gold beads, but to the present time nothing has been discovered in any way resembling the remarkably minute beads from the region of La Tolita.

A number of beads were collected on the Sinu river, Colombia, two of which are illustrated in fig. 62. They are crudely made of thin sheet-gold rolled into tubular form. As may be seen in the illustration, the ends are turned in,

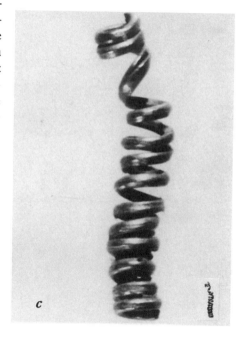

Fig. 57.—Beads made of spirally twisted gold wire. Ecuador. Enlarged and actual sizes. (1/7448).

either to eliminate the sharp edges or for ornamentation. The lengthwise joints are crudely made and seem to have been slightly fused.

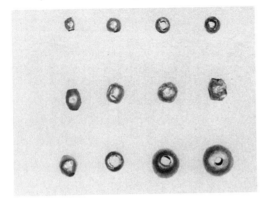

Five other tubular beads from the same region show a highly advanced degree of the goldsmith's art (fig. 63). They are half an inch long and a quarter of an inch in diameter. An inner tube of very thin gold forms the foundation for two whorls of a continuous wire, and a wire wrapped around

FIG. 58.—Spheroidal gold beads. Ecuador. (1/7434).

spirally at each end of the tube. There are indications that the parts were held together by fusing. One of the beads of this group, however, instead of having a spiral wire at each end has a three-strand braided wire wrapped once around. This feature exhibits a remark-

FIG. 59.—Spherical gold beads with a collar around the perforations. Ecuador. (10/9925).

FIG. 60.—Spherical gold beads with pressed designs. Ecuador. (10/9957).

able piece of work. The braiding is so close and tight that it seems hardly possible that this could have been accomplished with metal wires. The ends of one of these braided bands are so well brought together that the joint is not visible.

In strong contrast are some tubular beads from Bocas del Toro, Chiriqui, Panama (fig. 64). These are made of hammered sheet-gold with unevenly cut overlapping edges along the lengthwise joint, and with no attempt at fusion or other process for making a tight joint.

A very fine-grained pottery has been used for making the three well-shaped spherical beads shown in fig. 65, from the region of the Ulua river, Honduras. They are covered with a thin sheet of gold.

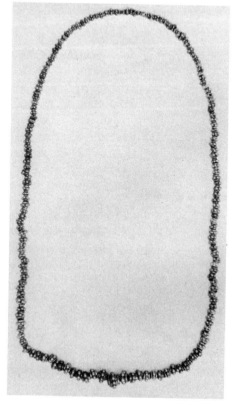

FIG. 62.—Tubular beads of thin sheet-gold, from Sinu river, Colombia. (5/3983).

FIG. 61.—Necklace of gold beads. (1/1229). See fig. 52 for detail of beads.

FIG. 63.—Tubular gold beads with wire ornamentation, from Sinu river, Colombia. (5/3982).

A micrometric reading gives two one-thousandths of an inch thickness for a fragment of the covering. The gold has been applied and made to adhere in a way that not a trace of a joint is visible. The surface appearance suggests burnishing, which might have been done after fusion to obliterate overlapping joints and uneven places; but this is conjectural. How this remarkable piece of work was accomplished must remain a mystery. Reference to ancient Mexican clay beads covered with gold-leaf has been made by Saville.[15]

---

[15] Saville, M. H., Goldsmith's Art in Ancient Mexico, *Ind. Notes and Monogr., Mus. Amer. Ind., Heye Found.*, misc. 7, 1920, p. 17.

Examples of gold beads from Florida in the Museum collections are shown, actual size, in fig. 66. They are nearly solid and appear to have been made somewhat after the manner of spun metal. It is possible that in such cases a piece of gold was drilled and put on a spindle of some kind which could be revolved, and while revolving, instead of heavy pressure being applied as in the case of spun metal, the piece of gold was hammered into shape and the hammer marks afterward removed with some abrasive material. The large oblate spheroidal bead on its end in the illustration shows where the gold has been beaten out and over the core-like center, spreading a thin

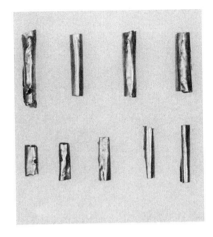

Fig. 64.—Tubular gold beads from Bocas del Toro, Panama. (8200).

sheet into the required bead form. The smaller bead in the center of the group shows the effect that might be produced by hammering and revolving, but in this example the gold has not been spread so much as in the larger one. The two barrel-shape beads were made in the same manner.

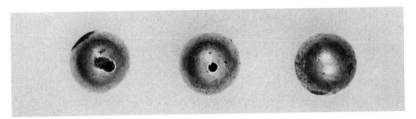

Fig. 65.—Gold-covered earthenware beads from Honduras. (6/1293).

From the Valley of Mexico there is a bead in the form of a human skull (fig. 67, a). It is of solid gold, with the perforation made from side to side, and is seven-sixteenths of an inch long.

A bead of unusual workmanship is shown in fig. 67, b, which is of an inferior quality of gold cast in a mold. The metal is very thin, and the design is composed of eight spiral discs with rings at each

end and one in the middle. This is an exceptionally fine piece of casting. A translation of
the Nahuatl text describing the methods employed
by the Aztecs in making molds and casting gold,
recorded by Sahagun, is to be found in Saville's
work above cited. The specimen illustrated was
found in the Magdalena valley, Colombia, where

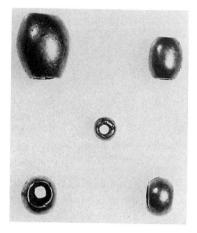

FIG. 67.—a,
Gold bead in the
form of a hu-
man skull, from
Mexico. b, Cast
gold bead from
C o l o m b i a.
(7035, 10/2603).

FIG. 66.—Gold beads from Florida.
(1/7967, 68, 71, 75, 76).

it is very probable the ancient goldsmiths employed a method similar
to that described by Sahagun.

BEADS OF SILVER

A number of necklaces recently collected consist of beads made of
flattened silver wire bent around an implement resembling a knitting-
needle. The ends are brought very close together, evidently with
pliers or a vise-like tool, and then hammered and rubbed until the
joints were almost obscured. Many of the beads have been shaped
into a flattened spherical form. A few of the larger ones are barrel-
shape, some are hammered four-sided or nearly square, while others
are of a short tubular form. One of the strings has a number of gold
beads inserted at intervals of about six inches; these are made of a
flattened wire in the same manner as those of silver, with no solder or
fusing at the joints. There are seven strings of these beads, each
about nine feet long, containing sixteen beads to the inch, with an

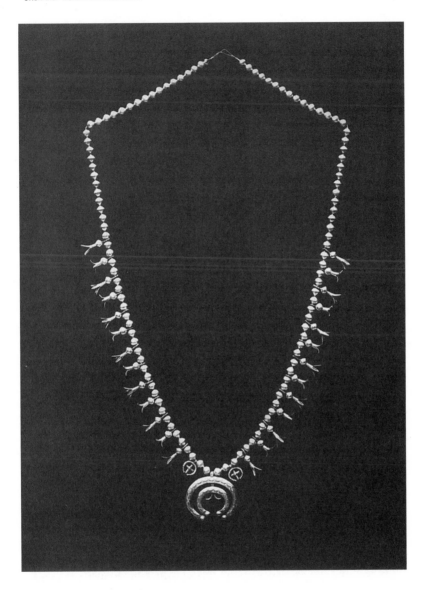

NECKLACE OF SILVER MADE BY THE NAVAHO.   (6/2129)

average of three-thirtyseconds of an inch in diameter. A few glass beads are interspersed. These are the product of the Araucanian Indians of Chile.

During the last half-century Navaho silversmiths have produced, among other ornaments, a distinctive form of necklace composed of spherical beads and pendants. Pl. X illustrates one of these typical necklaces. Distributed through about half of the length of the necklace are a number of flower-shape pendants with two beads between the pendants, and two crescentic ornaments, one within the other, are placed centrally in pendant form. Such necklaces have found favor also among the Pueblo Indians. The floral pendants are said by the Hopi to represent squash-blossoms, which to them are an emblem of fertility.[16]

Mexican pesos formerly furnished the silver, which was melted and run into molds made of easily worked sandstone. The beads, however, were not cast, but were made of two cup-shape pieces soldered together. The coins were annealed and hammered into thin sheets, discs of the required size were cut from the sheet-silver, and were shaped with die and matrix. Before they acquired more suitable equipment the Navaho and Pueblos employed as a die the rounded head of a bolt or other suitable piece of iron; the matrix is preferably a depression in the end grain of a piece of hard wood, just the size and shape required for the half of a bead. After being annealed the silver becomes somewhat softened and yields more readily during the shaping process. A disc is laid over the matrix and driven into the depression with the die and a hammer, which produces the cup-shape half of a bead. The edges, unavoidably rough and uneven, are ground and smoothed on a flat piece of sandstone. Perforations are made in the cups and afterward they are placed on a stiff wire in pairs forming globes, with their edges pressed closely together and secured with wrappings of fine wire. A mixture of borax and saliva forms the flux with small fragments of silver, which is applied to the joints for soldering the sections together. A number of beads so arranged are placed in a fire and the temperature raised to a sufficient degree with bellows to make the solder run and hold the edges together. Irregularities are filed off and the beads are polished. The floral pendant consists of a bead with four petals and a perforated shank. The petals are cast, and with the shank are soldered to the

---

[16] On the age of silverworking among the Navaho and Pueblos, see Hodge, F. W., in *El Palacio,* vol. xxv, nos. 14–17, Santa Fe, N. Mex., Oct. 6–27, 1928.

bead. The beads in the necklace illustrated are seven-sixteenths of an inch in diameter; the length of the string is twenty-six inches. The crescentic appendage is cast and bears a stamped design. The stamps are made of any suitably shaped piece of steel or iron with a pattern cut in one end. Many such implements of different designs may be found in a silversmith's kit. With a hammer the various patterns are stamped into the silver. The artist is not alone dependent on the stamps, for some of the ornamentation is produced with a graving tool often made of a piece of a three-cornered file with its end ground to a fine cutting point. This they use just as a civilized engraver would do. All this excellent work is accomplished by the Navaho without the aid of a measure or an instrument of precision.

Dr. Washington Matthews [17] has presented a detailed description of the methods employed by Navaho silversmiths in the manufacture of a wide variety of silver ornaments.

BEADS OF COPPER

Copper was used to some extent by Indians in the manufacture of utilitarian objects and ornaments, including beads. A great quantity of the metal was available in the Lake Superior region, although native copper is found also in Virginia, North Carolina, Tennessee, Arizona, New Mexico, Nova Scotia, and other localities. Beads of copper have been found in nearly all these areas, and in other parts where either the raw material or the finished articles must have been imported from various sources. A number of copper beads from Nova Scotia and New Brunswick have been recorded, and Prof. F. W. Putnam found one on Prince Edward Island.[18] These in all probability were made from the copper found in the respective regions.

FIG. 68.—Bead of laminated copper from Caney Fork, DeKalb county, Tenn. ¾. (4/7983).

Specimens from Tennessee include a cylindrical bead (fig. 68) which tapers from the center toward each end. Its size is three and three-eighths inches long and about five-eighths of an inch in maximum diameter. It was made from a copper nugget, hammered thin, then rolled and hammered

---

[17] *Second Ann. Rep. Bur. Ethn., 1881–82,* Washington, 1883.
[18] Putnam, F. W., Shell Heap on Prince Edward Island, *Amer. Antiquarian,* Jan.–Feb., 1896.

TUBULAR COPPER BEADS FROM HEWLETT, LONG ISLAND, NEW YORK. (8/3738)

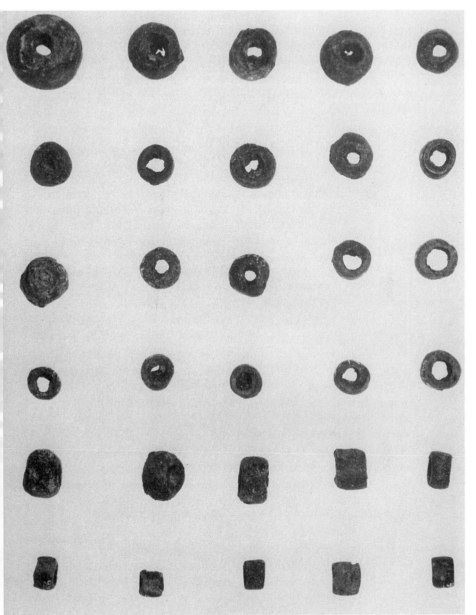

FLATTENED SPHERICAL BEADS OF COPPER FROM HEWLETT, LONG ISLAND, NEW YORK. ACTUAL SIZE. (8/3746)

into shape. Though badly corroded, the laminations are distinct and indicate definitely the mode of manufacture. Other beads from Tennessee, of tubular form but having parallel sides, are made from sheet-copper rolled into tubes of a single thickness of metal, with the edges slightly overlapping. These were probably made from copper obtained from early colonists in the form of kettles. These beads vary in size from a quarter of an inch to nearly two inches long and about a quarter of an inch in diameter.

A burial at Hewlett, Long Island, yielded two hundred or more beads of varying shapes and sizes. A number of the tubular form were included (Pl. XI), but corrosion was so far advanced that it is difficult to determine how these were made. Some of them at least have the appearance of being other than rolled sheet-metal, and are probably of European production. A number of flattened spherical beads were also with the burial (Pl. XIA); their general appearance is such as to suggest that they were European trade articles.

Fig. 69.— Copper bead from Niagara county, New York. Enlarged from ¾₄ in. (8/221).

The smallest copper beads brought to our notice are some on the original string, which has been preserved by the action of the copper salts on the fiber. An enlarged drawing (fig. 69) shows how they are made of small strips of the metal bent in tubular form with the edges brought together on an even plane. They were found with a burial near Lewiston, Niagara county, New York, and are three sixty-fourths of an inch in diameter. With them were found, also on the original string, some beads which are about twice as large, the two sizes being on separate strings. From a nearby locality a number of tubular objects, presumably beads, some of copper, others of brass, were gathered. These range in size from three-quarters of an inch to four and a half inches in length, and three-sixteenths to half an inch in diameter. These tubular objects are not so well made; the edges are irregular and overlap. The sheet-metal of which the larger ones are made, it is safe to say, was supplied by white people, and the even thickness of the edges of the smaller ones suggests the same origin for their material.

A necklace and a breast-ornament of copper from one

Fig. 70.— Bead made of flattened brass wire spirally twisted. Actual size. (13/7862).

of the Salish tribes of British Columbia are composed of a number
of long brass beads (fig. 70) made of wire which has been hammered flat and twisted spirally. The drawing shows their average size. Some of them have parallel sides instead of the tapering
ends shown in the drawing. Glass beads and seeds are interspersed.

WAMPUM

Under the classification of shell beads, perhaps those commonly
known as wampum may be considered the most important. During
the early days of white settlement in the northern continent wampum
was a recognized medium of exchange, or, when arranged on strings
in a particular order as to color, served in the conveyance of intertribal messages, or, when woven into a form known as belts, played
an important part in the ratification of treaties. In personal adornment the belts were very effective. Woven into the form of collars,
or on strings as necklaces, ear-pendants, or wristlets, they were more
commonly used.

The wampum to be discussed in this section is to be understood as
having the form of small cylindrical shell beads, averaging about a
quarter of an inch in length by an eighth of an inch in diameter—not
the discoidal beads found at prehistoric sites, although these may have
functioned in a somewhat similar way. The discoidal type of beads
still survives, and in some localities they are called wampum and are
used to some extent as money. But the wampum in mind is the
cylindrical kind which was made in two colors, white and purple.
The quahog, or hard-clam (*Venus mercenaria*), furnished extensively
the material for the manufacture of both colors of wampum, although
other shells of a suitable nature, such as the columellæ of the conch,
were used for the white beads. Some exception, it might be added,
has been taken to the use of the quahog-shell as not being thick enough
for making the dark beads. The reason, perhaps, is because the
necessary large clams are infrequently found among our present food
supply. The large clam is too old and tough for food, the smaller,
younger clams being the only ones found marketable; consequently
we see little or nothing of the larger clams and therefore find it difficult to imagine a shell thick enough for wampum-making. Beauchamp,[19] however, illustrates a fragment in which the purple part of
the shell is three-eighths of an inch thick.

[19] Beauchamp, W. M., Wampum and Shell Articles, *Bull. 41, N. Y. State
Mus.*, Albany, 1901.

Wampum is mentioned in the records of many early travelers in North America, but their references bear chiefly on its origin, and only vaguely on the mode of manufacture, the materials used, its uses and value.

According to Loskiel—

Wampom is an Iroquois word meaning a muscle. A number of these muscles strung together is called a *string of wampom*. . . . Before the Europeans came to North America, the Indians used to make their strings of wampom chiefly of small pieces of wood of equal size, stained either black or white. Few were made of muscles which were esteemed very valuable and difficult to make; for, not having proper tools, they spent much time in finishing them, and yet their work had a clumsy appearance. But the Europeans soon contrived to make strings of wampom, both neat and elegant, and in great abundance. The Indians immediately gave up the use of the old wooden substitutes for wampom, and procured those made of muscles, which, though fallen in price, were always accounted valuable.[20]

Closely following that of Loskiel, Isaac Weld's reference to wampum is of interest:

The wampum is formed of the inside of the clam shell, a large sea shell bearing some similitude to that of a scallop, which is found on the coasts of New England and Virginia. The shell is sent in its original rough state to England, and there cut into small pieces, exactly similar in shape and size to the modern glass bugles worn by ladies, which little bits of shell constitute wampum. There are two sorts of wampum, the white and the purple; the latter is most esteemed by the Indians, who think a pound weight of it equally valuable with a pound of silver. . . .

The use of wampum appears to be very general amongst the Indian nations, but how it became so, is a question that would require discussion, for it is well known that they are a people obstinately attached to old customs, and that they would not therefore be apt to adopt, on the most grand and solemn occasion, the use of an article they had never seen until brought to them by strangers; at the same time it seems wholly impossible that they should ever have been able to have made wampum from the clam shell for themselves; they fashion the bowls of tobacco pipes, indeed, from stone, in a very curious manner, and with astonishing accuracy, considering that they use no other instrument than a common knife, but then the stone which they commonly carve thus is of a very soft kind; the clam shell, however, is exceedingly hard, and to bore and cut it into such small pieces as are necessary to form wampum, very fine tools would be wanting.

[20] Loskiel, G. H., History of the Mission of the United Brethren among the Indians of North America, pt. 1, p. 26, London, 1794.

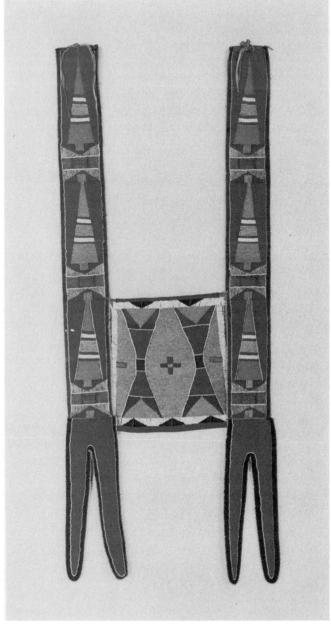

HORSE'S BREAST ORNAMENT. CROW, MONTANA. (20/7717) 42″ LONG

(See inside front cover for color version.)

Probably they made some use of the clam shell, and endeavoured to reduce it to as small bits as they could with their rude instruments before we came amongst them, but on finding that we could cut it so much more neatly than they could, laid aside the wampum before in use for that of our manufacture.[21]

Lawson,[22] writing of the manufacture of wampum in the South, states:

If this *Wampum Peak* be black or purple, as some Part of that Shell is, then it is twice the Value. This the *Indians* grind on Stones and other things till they make it current, but the Drilling is the most difficult to the *English*men, which the *Indians* manage with a Nail stuck in a Cane or Reed. Thus they roll it continually on their Thighs with their Right-hand, holding the Bit of Shell with their left, so in time they drill a Hole quite through it, which is a very tedious Work.

In an early record of wampum in New England, by Roger Williams,[23] giving its value as a medium of exchange, he writes:

The Indians are ignorant of Europes Coyne; yet they have given a name to ours, and call it Monèash from the English money.

Their owne is of two sorts; one white, which they make of the stem or stocke of the Periwincle, which they call Meteaûhock, when all the shell is broken off: and of this sort six of their small Beads (which they make with holes to string the bracelets) are currant with the English for a Peny.

The second is black, inclining to blew, which is made of the shell of a fish, which some English call Hens, Poquaûhock, and of this sort three make an English peny.

They that live upon the Sea side generally make of it, and as many make as will.

There seems to have been considerable fluctuation in values during the period of Roger Williams' observation, for he states:

One fathom of this their stringed money, now worth of the English but five shillings (sometimes more) some few yeeres since was worth nine, and sometimes ten shillings per Fathome. . . .

They hang these strings of money about their necks and wrists; as also upon the necks and wrists of their wives and children.[24]

---

[21] Weld, Isaac, Travels through the States of North America and the Provinces of Upper and Lower Canada during the Years 1795, 1796, 1797, pp. 390–391, London, 1799.

[22] Lawson, John, History of Carolina, p. 194, London, 1714.

[23] Williams, R., A Key into the Language of America (1643), p. 128, Providence, 1827.

[24] Ibid., pp. 129, 131.

Referring to the Indians of Virginia, Beverley [25] wrote:

The *Indians* had nothing which they reckoned Riches, before the *English* went among them, except *Peak, Roenoke,* and such like trifles made out of the *Cunk*-shell. These past with them instead of Gold and Silver, and serv'd them both for Money, and Ornament. . . .

Peak is of two sorts, or rather of two colours, for both are made of one Shell, tho of different parts; one is a dark Purple Cylinder, and the other a white; they are both made in size, and figure alike, and commonly much resembling the *English Buglas,* but not so transparent nor so brittle. They are wrought as smooth as Glass, being one third of an inch long, and about a quarter, diameter, strung by a hole drill'd thro the Center. The dark colour is the dearest, and distinguish'd by the name of *Wampom Peak.* The *English*-men that are call'd *Indian* Traders, value the *Wampom Peak,* at eighteen pence *per* Yard, and the white *Peak* at nine pence. The Indians also make Pipes of this, two or three inches long, and thicker than ordinary, which are much more valuable. They also make *Runtees* of the same Shell, and grind them as smooth as *Peak.* These are either large like an Oval Bead, and drill'd the length of the Oval, or else they are circular and flat, almost an inch over, and one third of an inch thick, and drill'd edgeways. Of this Shell they also make round Tablets of about four inches diameter, which they polish as smooth as the other, and sometimes they etch or grave thereon, Circles, Stars, a Half Moon, or any other figure suitable to their fancy. These they wear instead of Medals before or behind their Neck, and use the *Peak, Runtees* and Pipes for Coronets, Bracelets, Belts or long Strings hanging down before the Breast, or else they lace their Garments with them, and adorn their *Tomahawks,* and every other thing that they value.

They have also another sort which is as current among them, but of far less value; and this is made of the Cockle shell, broke into small bits with rough edges, drilled through in the same manner as Beads, and this they call *Roenoke,* and use it as the *Peak.*

These quotations, excepting those from Weld and Beverley, provide no very definite description as to the shape of the wampum, whether it was discoidal or tubular. However, the fact is well established that few tubular beads have been found on prehistoric sites. In later burials, on the other hand, great numbers have been found, but always associated more or less with objects of European origin. It is therefore safe to assume that the particular style of wampum under discussion was mostly made after the introduction of iron by

---

[25] Beverley, Robert, History and Present State of Virginia, bk. III, chap. 12, pp. 58, 59, London, 1705.

Europeans, for this metal must have been used for making the perforations. There are a few exceptions, perhaps, where small cylindrical shell beads have been perforated with other than iron or steel drills, but the drillings are invariably large in proportion to the size of the bead, and as a rule taper toward the center. In the case of discoidal beads the drilling is a simple matter: the perforations are made in the center of a disc, and according to the thickness of the shell may be made from either one or both sides, while a small angular stone point is easily maintained in the shaft of a drill. Beads of this class have been found in quantities on prehistoric sites, so that it is reasonable to suppose that this wampum, or its equivalent under various names, was the kind the earliest explorers found in use among the Indians, rather than what is commonly known today as wampum.

The drilling of cylindrical beads, the typical wampum, examples of which are shown in the illustrations, could hardly have been done with a stone point, because the perforations are long and narrow, and a point of stone of sufficient length would be difficult to make, and if made, the least deviation from the line of drilling would break the drill, if not the bead. Copper implements of a suitable character have not been found in numbers sufficient to suggest their use for this purpose. The use of reeds or of like material in conjunction with sand and water would seem most improbable when we consider the prodigious quantities of wampum that exist and the time required to drill a bead by such means.

For the purpose of examining the shape and general appearance of tubular drillings a series of excellent X-ray photographs have been prepared by Dr. Elsie Fox, of New York City, an expert in that line, who kindly volunteered her services toward solving this interesting problem.

Pl. XIV, a, illustrates a fragment of a wampum belt, and b is an X-ray photograph of the same specimen, showing the drillings of the beads. It may be seen that many of the perforations have been made from each end of the bead, showing clearly where the drill has not been held true and the meeting points have not come exactly together. Others have evidently been drilled from one end.

Pl. XV, a, is a photograph of a portion of another belt, with an accompanying X-ray print (b) showing a marked improvement in the drillings, which evidently were made from one end and are parallel with the sides of the beads. The general appearance of this work

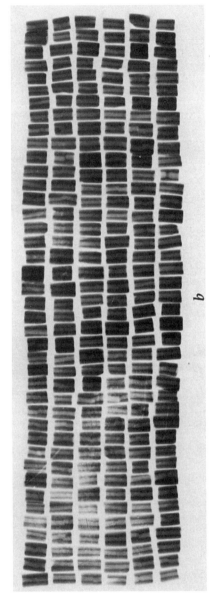

a, FRAGMENT OF A WAMPUM BELT OF THE SENECA OF CATTARAUGUS RESERVATION, NEW YORK. *b*, X-RAY PHOTOGRAPH OF THE SAME,

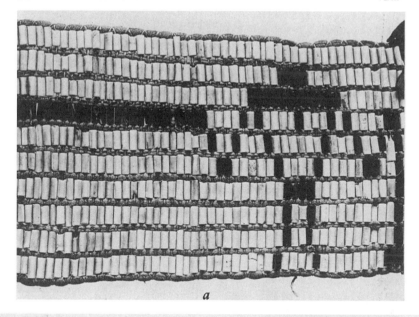

a, PART OF A WAMPUM BELT OF THE SENECA OF GRAND RIVER RESERVATION, ONTARIO. *b*, X-RAY PHOTOGRAPH OF THE SAME, SHOWING THE DRILLING OF THE BEADS. (10/4263)

(X-RAY PHOTOGRAPH BY DR. ELSIE FOX)

suggests that both the beads and the drill were held in such manner that there should be no deviation in the course of the drill. Appliances of this kind, however crude, may be classed under the head of machinery. The device for holding the bead, if only a cleft stick, is a form of vise or clamp, while braces to keep the drill-shaft running true are nothing more nor less than a lathe head in embryo. Taking for granted that such devices were used, we have truly machine-made beads.

Fig. 71 is an X-ray photograph of an unusually fine string of beads, in regard to both the diameter of the beads and the drilling. The perforations are true and of uniform size, as though one drill had

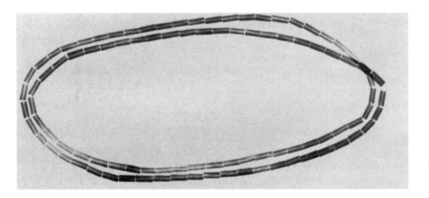

Fig. 71.—X-ray photograph of an Iroquois wampum necklace from Brantford, Ontario. (1/2673). Photograph by Dr. Elsie Fox.

been used to complete the work. There is no reason why the Indians, with their well-known ingenuity, should not have contrived some mechanical means for drilling the cylindrical wampum so perfectly, after they had been supplied with iron or steel, without suggestions from Europeans, who at an early date commenced the manufacture of wampum when it became an accepted medium of exchange. An interesting account of the commercial manufacture of wampum is given by Barber and Howe,[26] as follows:

Wampum, or Indian money, is to the present day made in this [Bergen] county, and sold to the Indian traders of the far west. It has been manufactured, by the females in this region, from very early times for the Indians; and as every thing connected with this interesting race is destined,

[26] Barber and Howe, Historical Collections of the State of New Jersey, p. 72, New York, 1840.

at no distant period, to exist only in history, we annex a description of the manufacture.

The wampum is made from the thick and blue part of sea-clamshells. The process is simple, but requires a skill only attained by long practice. The intense hardness and brittleness of the material render it impossible to produce the article by machinery alone. It is done by wearing or grinding the shell. The first process is to split off the thin part with a light sharp hammer. Then it is clamped in the sawed crevice of a slender stick, held in both hands, and ground smooth on a grindstone, until formed into an eight-sided figure, of about an inch in length and nearly half an inch in diameter; when it is ready for boring. The shell then is inserted into another piece of wood, sawed similarly to the above, but fastened firmly to a bench of the size of a common stand. One part of the wood projects over the bench, at the end of which hangs a weight, causing the sawed orifice to close firmly upon the shell inserted on its under side, and to hold it firmly, as in a vice, ready for drilling. The drill is made from an untempered handsaw. The operator grinds the drill to a proper shape, and tempers it in the flame of a candle. A rude ring, with a groove on its circumference, is put on it; around which the operator, (seated in front of the fastened shell,) curls the string of a common hand-bow. The boring commences, by nicely adjusting the point of the drill to the centre of the shell; while the other end is braced against a steel plate, on the breast of the operator. About every other sweep of the bow, the drill is dexterously drawn out, cleaned of the shelly particles by the thumb and finger, above which drops of water from a vessel fall down and cool the drill; which is still kept revolving, by the use of the bow with the other hand, the same as though it were in the shell. This operation of boring is the most difficult of all, the peculiar motion of the drill rendering it hard for the breast; yet it is performed with a rapidity and grace interesting to witness. Peculiar care is observed, lest the shell burst from heat caused by friction. When bored half way, the wampum is reversed, and the same operation repeated. The next process is the finishing. A wire, about twelve inches long, is fastened at one end to a bench. Under and parallel to the wire is a grindstone, fluted on its circumference, hung a little out of the centre, so as to be turned by a treadle moved with the foot. The left hand grasps the end of the wire, on which are strung the wampum, and, as it were, wraps the beads around the fluted or hollow circumference of the grindstone. While the grindstone is revolving, the beads are held down on to it, and turned round by a flat piece of wood held in the right hand, and by the grinding soon become round and smooth. They are then strung on hempen strings, about a foot in length. From five to ten strings are a day's work for a female. They are sold to the country merchants for twelve and a half cents a string, always command cash, and constitute the support of many poor and worthy families.

John W. Campbell was born July 31, 1746, and early in life settled at Pascack where he established a wampum factory and for years conducted an extensive business, supplying the United States Indian agents and traders of the day with " Indian money." His descendants, until quite recently, continued its manufacture.

Seven strings of the Campbell wampum are illustrated in Pl. XVI. The strings are as described in the foregoing citation, being about 12 inches long, while the beads are of lengths varying from about half an inch to seven-eighths of an inch, and of a uniform diameter of three-sixteenths of an inch. Only a small number of the beads, however, are less than seven-eighths of an inch in length. These are much larger in every respect than those made commercially before the Campbell factory commenced operations. No beads of such size appear in any of the known wampum belts. It is not to be supposed that the Campbells were pioneers in the industry, for, as Beauchamp writes,[27] " the Dutch had learned to make wampum by improved methods, having used it from the first, and the Iroquois bought large quantities."

There is no doubt that the Indians made quantities of wampum, as their demand for muxes (awls) and needles is noted in early records.

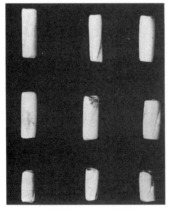

FIG. 72.—W a m p u m made without steel tools: found at Lewiston, New York. Actual size. (8/8550).

Many of these articles were given as part payment by the Colonists for Indian lands. To quote Roger Williams, " Before ever they had awle blades from Europe, they made shift to bore this their shell money with stones." [28]

In the Indian deed for Huntington, Long Island, dated 1650, are mentioned " 30 muxes and 30 needles." Among the articles given for East Hampton, Long Island, in 1648, were one hundred muxes. The deed for Mastic Neck, Brookhaven, Long Island, in 1657, specifies, among other things, " forty needles and forty muxes." In the records of many other transactions muxes are mentioned, attesting to the fact that those implements were in great demand by the Indians.

[27] Beauchamp, W. M., History of the New York Iroquois, *Bull. 78, N. Y. State Mus.*, Albany, 1905.
[28] Williams, Roger, op. cit., p. 130.

REGULATION BUNCH OF WAMPUM PREPARED FOR TRADE BY WHITE MANUFACTURERS
IN NEW JERSEY. (2/9813)

With reference to the age of this particular form of wampum, there seems to be conclusive evidence that it was not made until after the arrival of Europeans. No doubt many of the kind shown in fig. 72 were in use by the natives before they came in contact with white men, but all that have been recovered are larger and coarser than those which were made with the aid of steel drills. Much of the coarser kind has been found on prehistoric sites, but never any of the smaller variety. An expression of opinion on this point was asked of three prominent archeologists who have made many field investigations in the East. Their statements are herein quoted. Mr. Arthur C. Parker, Director of the Rochester Municipal Museum, states:

During the past twenty-two years I have examined numerous Indian village and burial sites of the several cultures in New York and northern Pennsylvania. I have given pre-colonial, otherwise pre-contact, sites considerable care in this area, recording the range of artifacts found upon each site examined.

I have found shell beads, shaped as spheroids, ovals, and disks in village-sites and graves in certain pre-contact Algonkian sites, and I have found the same type of beads in pre-contact Iroquoian sites and also long heavy cylindrical beads made from the columella of the *Pyrula* (*Busycon*), but I have never found the small cylindrical beads such as are found in wampum belts and strings in any of these early sites. Where small cylindrical beads have been found they are at least three times the diameter of the historic wampum bead and made of a different variety of shell.

Historic wampum, such as is known as 'belt wampum,' appears abundantly in sites of about 1650. Sites of twenty to fifty years earlier have it only rarely or sparingly, but by the middle of the 17th century it appears in great quantities, many graves yielding from a pint to four quarts of it. It continued in abundance among the historic Iroquois until about 1800. Its use by them after this period was confined mostly to strings and belts used in council and ceremony. Occasionally a belt or string was buried with the dead, but glass beads gradually drove out wampum as a clothing decoration and its growing scarcity prevented its use as a burial tribute.

Mr. M. R. Harrington, formerly of the Museum of the American Indian, Heye Foundation, now Director of Research in the Southwest Museum, Los Angeles, has done extensive archeological work in the region of New York. He writes:

As to wampum, I think that cylindrical shell beads, mostly white and made from *Fulgur* cones, and slightly larger than standard wampum, were

made in fair quantity before the coming of the whites; but that the great
development of what we call wampum began in early Colonial days, after
the Indians secured steel drills.   On Long Island, at Dosoris, near Glen
Cove, to be exact, I found *Fulgur* cones (columellæ) that had been ground
into slender cylinders and marked into lengths suitable for wampum, but
no finished beads.   On Tennessee river I found shell beads like coarse
white wampum, some of them on sites where no white man's products appeared, and others, very similar, on sites where a few trade articles were
seen.   The Long Island site mentioned above showed nothing of European
origin.

Quoting the late Alanson Skinner, also of the Museum of the
American Indian:

I have never seen a single wampum bead from any prehistoric Iroquois
site that I have visited in New York, Canada, or Pennsylvania.   On the
contrary, they are exceedingly abundant in the graves, and even on the
surface, of the historic towns.   On prehistoric Onondaga sites in Jefferson
county, we found disc beads of dark steatite quite commonly, and more
rarely, similar beads of shell, and I think, bone.

In addition to these statements we quote from Beauchamp,[29] as
follows:

I have mentioned the lack of wampum among the early New York Iroquois, as proof that they had not reached the sea, but it was not abundant
even on the coast in prehistoric times.   On early Iroquois sites it is not
found, nor anything resembling it.

These statements are presented to correct an impression which has
prevailed, more or less, that the regulation belt wampum was made
and used by the Indians in prehistoric times.

The uses of wampum have been described by Dr. Frank G. Speck
in his memoir on The Functions of Wampum Among the Eastern
Algonkian.[30]

WAMPUM-MAKING TOOLS

A series of implements necessary for making wampum has been
brought together for the Museum by Mr. Carl F. Schondorf, of
Paterson, New Jersey, who for a number of years has been deeply
interested in the subject and has succeeded not only in gathering the

---

[29] Beauchamp, W. M., History of the New York Iroquois, *Bull. 78, N. Y.
State Mus.,* Albany, 1905.
[30] *Mem. Amer. Anthr. Asso.,* vol. VI, no. 1, 1919.

actual tools but in recording some authentic information on the manufacture of wampum from descendants of at least two of the families
who made it for the Campbells, who in turn supplied Western traders
with the beads. The tools were procured from descendants of Jane
Ann Bell and Fowler Bross, both noted in their day for their ability
in beadmaking.

According to these people the quahog, or hard-clam shell (*Venus
mercenaria*), was used exclusively for the purple wampum. The
shells were secured in quantities by the Campbells, who sold them to
the beadmakers.

The tools, as shown in the illustration (fig. 73), consist of a short-
handled double-bladed adz (*a*) used in connection with a short chisel-

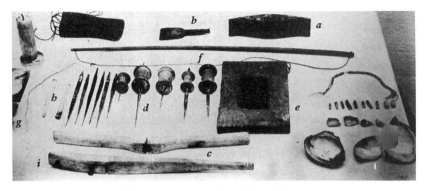

Fig. 73.—Tools for making " Dutch " wampum.

like implement (*b*) for cutting the purple edge of the shells into
pieces of required size, which afterward were roughly ground into
octagonal shape on a grindstone. The implement for holding the
fragment of shell (*c*) during this operation is made from a hickory
stick about fourteen inches long, an inch wide, and three-quarters of
an inch thick, tapering from the center to about a quarter of an inch
thick at each end. A cleft was made across the middle of the stick,
leaving enough of the wood to form a hinge for the two ends. The
elasticity of hickory permitted the cleft to spread apart and to hold
the fragment of shell to be shaped on the grindstone. This made a
very practical instrument for the purpose. Bearing down on both
ends of the stick closed the cleft so that the shell could not slip out
of place (fig. 74). After the shell was shaped, the ends were ground
square, held with the same implement (fig. 75).

Making the perforations was the next stage of manufacture. The drills (fig. 73, *d*) were made from saw-files. One end was carefully drawn out to a point an inch or an inch and a half long, and provided with a flat chisel-like cutting point. The opposite end is rounded to fit into a breast-plate (*e*). The drill was revolved with a bow (*f*) with the string wrapped around a common thread spool which was placed on the shaft of the drill near the rounded end.

FIG. 74.—Wampum making: Roughly shaping a piece of shell before drilling.

According to the beadmakers, the preparation of the drill was an important matter, as a poorly made instrument would split the shell while drilling or otherwise retard the production. The drawn-out point must be perfectly alined with the rest of the file forming the shaft, or spindle, the cutting edge a trifle broader than the diameter of that part forming the drill-shaft, to allow a clearance for the revolution of the drill and the accumulating shell particles during the process. The temper of the drill was finely adjusted in order that the cutting be subjected to as little interruption as possible.

During the operation of perforating, w a t e r was constantly applied with the fingers to keep the drill-point from get-

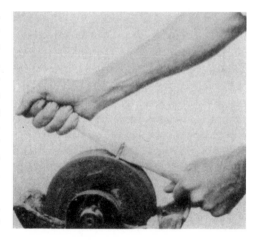

FIG. 75.—Wampum making: Squaring the ends of the shell by grinding.

ting hot and spoiling the temper. The points were frequently sharp-ened on a whetstone (fig. 73, g), and occasionally tempered. A candle was used to supply the heat, the flame being blown to the drill-point with a blowpipe (h) made from the stem of a clay pipe.

FIG. 76.—Wampum making: Perforating a roughly shaped bead.

While red-hot the point was quickly dipped into tallow, which gave it the requisite temper or hardness. During the drilling the piece of shell was held on a clamp (i) similar in form to that used to hold the shell while being roughly ground into shape, except that the cleft was cut nearer one end, rather than in the middle. The short end was screwed to the edge of a table or work-bench with the long end pro-jecting beyond the end of the table. A weight was attached to the end of the clamp with a string to close the cleft and thus hold the shell firmly (fig. 76). Generally the drilling was made from one direction, but an inexpert beadmaker might find it necessary to com-plete the perforation from the opposite end. After drilling a number of the beads, they were strung on a stiff wire, one end fastened to the work-bench or some other convenient place, while the other was held so that the beads might be rounded and finished on a grindstone.

The finished beads were assembled on strings about eleven inches long, containing about fifteen or twenty beads to a string, and were sold to the factory for about fifteen cents a string. White wampum, which was usually made from the columella of a conch, sold for about half that price. The methods employed for assembling the beads for their various uses are described on pages 78-80.

ODD FORMS AND MATERIALS

Seed Beads.—Besides animal and mineral substances used in the manufacture of beads, many kinds of seeds, especially those highly-colored varieties found in the tropics, were, and still are, perforated and strung for necklaces or attached to various objects for ornamental purposes. Some of the Californian tribes used great quantities of juniper-seeds for necklaces and for fringes of their ceremonial dresses; in addition they have ground the ends of pine-nuts so that there would be a lengthwise perforation. These have been used either alone or interspersed with the juniper-seeds. Similar seeds were used for necklaces by the Zuñi of New Mexico from ancient times until a couple of generations ago.

From caves in the Ozark mountains a Museum expedition conducted by Mr. M. R. Harrington recovered some Chickasaw plum-stones (*Prunus chicasa*) with their ends ground off evidently for the purpose of stringing. Also found were some very small white seeds, identified as those of false gromwell (*Onosmodium subsetosum*), which had been strung and were still on the original strings. A casual glance might give the impression that they were opaque white glass beads known to the trade in size as number 2/0. The end of these seeds have been ground off, rather than drilled, for the passage of a string.

A necklace made of lupine-seeds was found in a cave in Kane county, Utah, with another string of unidentified seeds; and a similar string was found in Grand gulch, in the same state. The presence of this material in the caves is ample evidence that the prehistoric peoples, among other things, used seeds for beads.

A necklace composed of silverberries (*Elæganus* sp.) was collected from one of the Apache tribes in New Mexico. And from the Chiricahua Apache in Oklahoma, a necklace of short perforated sections of a root considered by the Indians to be a potent medicine was obtained. Such specimens are by no means uncommon and many were regarded by the original owners as having efficacious medicinal properties.

The use of seeds as beads is well shown in Pl. XVII. The specimen here illustrated is one of a number collected from the Jivaro, one of the largest and most warlike tribes of South America whose territory includes many miles of unexplored country in the region of the rivers Upano-Santiago, Morona, and Pastaza in Ecuador and Peru. The object is a breast-ornament, worn by a man with other highly decorated objects on ceremonial occasions. It is made of palm-bark beaten into a soft cloth-like material of tan color. The ornamentation represents a face. The eyes, nose, mouth, cheeks, and eyebrows are of brilliant colored feathers, outlined with beads made of various seeds and sections of bird-bones. The uncovered parts of the bark cloth are colored with red paint to represent facial paintings, a customary practice among many tribes. The lower parts of the eyes, nose, and mouth, and the outer edge of the ornament, are fringed with threaded seeds. The ends of the fringe attached to the outer edge are further ornamented with half of a nut-shell and a colored feather. Between the eyes, at the apex of the nose, is the entire skin of a small bird, similar in appearance to the redwing blackbird of North America. Several Jivaro ornaments of this character in the Museum collections are made on a poorly tanned skin instead of on bark cloth; but taken together they may be said to be the most striking, so far as color is concerned, of any of the Museum's specimens.

Basketry Beads.—From the Wapisiana Indians of British Guiana was obtained a unique string of beads, each bead, globular in form, being made of basketry (fig. 77, *a*) consisting of narrow strips of palm-leaf cleverly woven with a circular opening at each extremity and the ends of the weaving strips concealed. The beads are strung on a native spun cotton cord with alternating short sections of bird-bone. The basketry beads are from a half to three-quarters of an inch in diameter.

Wooden Beads.—A necklace made by the Macoa of Venezuela consists of rectangular wooden beads varying from three-eighths to seven-eighths of an inch in length and about three-sixteenths of an inch in the square (fig. 77, *b*). Some are decorated with incised lines, others with notched corners.

Gum Beads.—About fifty beads made from a hard transparent gum, dark amber in color, were found in Clatsop county, Oregon. They are roughly made, rectangular in form, average about five-eighths of an inch wide by half an inch long and about three-sixteenths of an inch thick. The edges are irregularly faceted. Beads made of gum are not common, probably for the reason that such material is not durable.

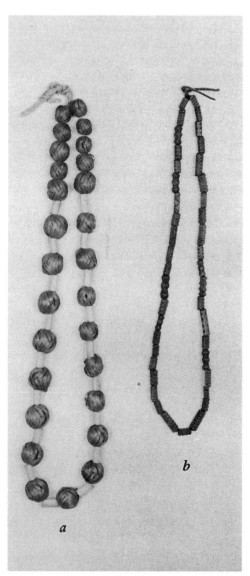

FIG. 77.—*a*, Necklace of basketry beads and sections of bird-bone; British Guiana. *b*, Necklace of incised wooden beads; Venezuela. (7/4936, 9/256).

Another necklace of gum or wax beads on the original string was obtained from natives in Santander, Colombia. The material has not been fully identified, but it is quite hard and tough, and in color is black and tan. While the material was soft, the two colors were twisted t o g e t h e r. in rather coarse bands, producing zebra-like stripes. The beads, or pendants, as their shape would denote, are of an elongate pear shape from five-eighths to three-quarters of an inch long and about a quarter of an inch in maximum diameter, tapering to a point with a lateral perforation at the smaller end.

Earthware Beads.— Two rather remarkable pottery beads of tubular form were brought to the Museum from Lara, Venezuela (fig. 78). One is three-quarters of an inch long, the other half an inch, both three-sixteenths of an inch in diameter. The clay of which they were made is of very fine texture, and has been given a burnished surface. The ends are rounded, and embellished with an indented line; the sides are ornamented with four rows of lengthwise punctate lines. These beads apparently were made on a round stem of some vegetal material, which was destroyed in the firing. The operation of firing produced a pleasing red-ochre color. Several other pottery beads of tubular form, also from Venezuela, are in the Museum collections. These, however, are without decoration; they measure an inch and a half to an inch and three-quarters long, about five-sixteenths of an inch in diameter, and are gray in color.

FIG. 78.— Tubular bead of pottery from Venezuela. Actual size. (4/8755).

Another odd form may be mentioned here. About one hundred and thirty imperforate objects which have been called beads were found at El Cayo and Wild Cane cay in British Honduras. They are made of pottery, are slightly flattened ovoid in shape, and vary from about half an inch to an inch and an eighth in length. Four of these specimens are illustrated in fig. 79. Some of them are grooved around the greater diameter, while others are notched at the ends. If these objects were used as beads they might have been effectively strung with a double string knotted between the beads. Their use as weights for weaving or as net-sinkers is extremely doubtful, as the material of which they are made is too light in weight for such purpose.

When one considers the incalculable amount of pottery that has been made by Indians, it is remarkable that so few earthenware beads have been found. One reason which may account for it is that much of the pottery-making clay was so coarse in texture that it would not afford a finished surface suitable for objects of a purely ornamental character. Some of the pottery of the Southwest, as well as of Mexico and Central America, is indeed of very fine, hard texture, capable of receiving a burnished surface. It would seem that beads of such material

FIG. 79.—Pottery beads grooved for stringing. British Honduras. (9/6411-9/6412).

could have been produced with much less effort than must have been expended on the great numbers made of other materials. A few globular beads of pottery, rather crudely made, from a quarter to five-eighths of an inch in diameter, were brought from Yucatan, and others were found at Hawikuh, New Mexico. These have not received any form of decoration, have a rough surface, and are dull gray in color, consequently they cannot be classed as objects of especial ornamental value.

Earthenware beads covered with gold have already been mentioned.

Beads of Dried Otter's Liver.—From the Winnebago the Museum has a string of yellow glass beads interspersed with small pieces of dried otter's liver which have been roughly shaped to resemble the beads in size. This was worn in the form of a necklace by a child as a charm against the ills common to childhood.

Native Manufacture of Glass Beads.—There are reports extant to the effect that some of the tribes of the upper Missouri made beads of glass obtained from traders or settlers. No examples of the work have at present been secured for the Museum's collection, but the existence of a single specimen is reported among the Arikara, which is the only piece so far known. However, it is so highly prized that there is little possibility that they will ever part with it.

According to the description of the process of manufacture, and of the paucity of examples of the work, it is safe to assume that very few such beads were made. The heat necessary for fusing glass to make a satisfactory bead could hardly be obtained in the manner described by the informant who furnished the following account given by Lewis and Clark in 1805 : [31]

Mr. Garrow a Frenchman who has lived many years with the Ricares & Mandans shewed us the process used by those Indians to make beads. the discovery of this art these nations are said to have derived from the Snake Indians who have been taken prisoners by the Ricaras. the art is kept a secret by the Indians among themselves and is yet known to but few of them. the Process is as follows.—Take glass of as many different colours as you think proper, then pound it as fine as possible, puting each colour in a seperate vessel. wash the pounded Glass in several waters throwing off the water at each washing, continue this opperation as long as the pounded glass stains or colours the water which is poured off and the residuum is then prepared for uce. you then provide an earthen pot of convenient size say of three gallons which will stand the fire; a platter

---

[31] Original Journals of the Lewis and Clark Expedition, vol. I, pp. 272–274, New York, 1904.

also of the same material sufficiently small to be admitted in the mouth of the pot or jar. the pot has a nitch in it's edge through which to watch the beads when in blast. You then provide some well seasoned clay with a proportion of sand sufficient to prevent it's becoming very hard when exposed to the heat. this clay must be tempered with water until it is about the consistency of common doe. of this clay you then prepare, a sufficient number of little sticks of the size you wish the hole through the bead, which you do by roling the clay on the palm of the hand with your finger. this done put those sticks of clay on the platter and expose them to red heat for a few minutes when you take them off and suffer them to cool. the pot is also heated to cles [cleanse] it perfectly of any filth it may contain. small balls of clay are also mad[e] of about an ounce weight which serve as a pedestal for a bead. these while soft ar destributed over the face of the platter at su[c]h distance from each other as to prevent the beads from touching. some little wooden paddles are now provided from three to four inches in length sharpened or brought to a point at the extremity of the handle. With this paddle you place in the palm of the hand as much of the wet pounded glass as is necessary to make the bead of the size you wish it. it is then arranged with the paddle in an oblong from [form], laying one of those little stick of clay crosswise over it; the pounded glass by means of the paddle is then roped in cilindrical form around the stick of clay and gently roled by motion of the hand backwards an forwards untill you get it as regular and smooth as you conveniently can. if you wish to introduce any other colour you now purforate the surface of the bead with the pointed end of your little paddle and fill up the cavity with other pounded glass of the colour you wish forming the whole as regular as you can. a hole is now made in the center of the little pedestals of clay with the handle of your shovel sufficiently large to admit the end of the stick of clay arround which the bead is formed. the beads are then arranged perpendicularly on their pedestals and little distance above them supported by the little sticks of clay to which they are attatched in the manner before mentioned. thus arranged the platter is deposited on burning coals or hot embers and the pot reversed with the apparture in its edge turned towards covers the whole. dry wood pretty much doated [doughted] is then plased arron [around] the pot in sush manner as compleatly to cover it. [It] is then set on fire and the opperator must shortly after begin to watch his beads through the apparture of the pot le[s]t they should be distroyed by being over heated. he suffers the beads to acquire a deepred heat from which when it passes in a small degree to a pailer or whitish red, or he discovers that the beads begin to become pointed at their extremities he removes the fire from about the pot and suffers the whole to cool gradually. the pot is then removed and the beads taken out. the clay which fills the hollow of the beads is picked out with an awl or nedle. the bead is then fit for uce. the Indians are extreemly fond of the large beads formed by this process. they use them as pendants to their years, or hair and sometimes wear them about their necks.

According to the statement of Lewis and Clark the informant " shewed us the process," but there is no evidence that they obtained and preserved a specimen, which is to be regretted. There are a few weak points in the description of the method. For example, the pounded colored glass would hardly be expected to stain or color the water in which it was washed, and in the absence of any statement to the contrary, we assume that the pulverized glass was made into a paste with water and rolled into form. There is room for doubt whether the paste would retain its form after the water had been driven out by the heat. But such discrepancies may have been due to lack of care in recording the procedure.

Catlin [32] also mentions the manufacture of glass beads by the Mandan and their exclusive possession of the art. Matthews,[33] however, says that the Arikara women also practised the art, and he thought that these peoples made " glazed earthen ornaments before the whites came among them."

Another reference to this art is given by Dr. George Bird Grinnell:

Long, long ago, we are told, the Cheyennes manufactured for themselves what might be called beads, but perhaps were small charms made of some vitrified substance—perhaps of pulverized glass—after the white people were met. Such beads are said to have been made within two or three generations. Many of them were fashioned in the shape of a lizard; that is, a four-legged object with a long tail and a small head. The ceremony connected with making such objects was secret, and he who wished to possess one was obliged to go to some person who himself had been taught the ceremony, and to ask that person to teach him how to make one. A payment was made for the service. It is believed that in old times, long before the whites came, these beads were made from the quartz sand found on ant-hills, and that this was melted in an earthen pot. The secret of making them now seems to be lost.

In later times they melted the glass, with which to make the beads, in the ladles used in melting lead for their bullets. These ornaments or charms were made in various shapes, often in the form of a lizard, as said, or flat on one side and round on the other. Sometimes they had a perforation through which a string might be passed; at other times merely

---

[32] Catlin, George, North American Indians, vol. II, p. 261, London, 1844.
[33] Matthews, Washington, Ethnography and Philology of the Hidatsa Indians, pp. 22–23, Washington, 1877.

a constriction between two ends about which a string was tied. The mold was made of clay.

The first European beads possessed by the Cheyennes were white, coarse, and imperfect in finish, but were highly valued. Few of these are now in existence.[34]

Other Aberrant Objects.—Among the odd forms are a number of gold objects found in the region of Sinu river, Colombia, four of which are pictured in fig. 80. They are of cast gold, in the form

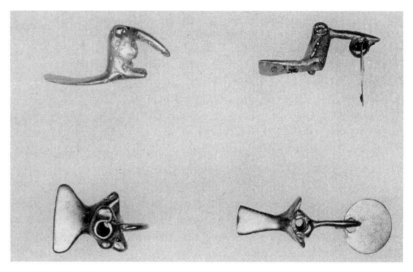

Fig. 80.—Bird-form gold objects from Colombia. (5/1971, 3961–62).

of birds, suggestive of the humming-bird. The perforations are through the head and lengthwise through the body. Some have a circular pendant of thin gold suspended near the extremity of the beak, and another has also a similar pendant attached to the tail. There is no positive reason for calling these objects beads; the perforations may have been made for some other purpose than the passage of a string.

Three other objects of similar form and size from Colombia are provided with ferrule-like appurtenances on which the birds stand as though perched on a branch, except that under ordinary circumstances a bird sits crosswise rather than lengthwise on a limb as in the case of these ornaments. The open end of the ferrules are at the

---

[34] Grinnell, Cheyenne Indians, vol. i, p. 223, New Haven, 1924.

extremities of the birds' tails, where it would be possible to insert a small rod or staff. The bodies of the birds are imperforate. Several massive gold objects in the Museum collections are made in the same manner, with ferrules large enough to admit a staff an inch or more in diameter. These in all probability were used ceremonially. It is possible that the smaller objects were made for some such purpose, although those we have called beads are provided with perforations which, from their size, would suggest the passage of a string rather than the insertion of a rod.

TRADE BEADS

Age and Distribution.—Early explorers in all parts of the world found beads of glass, porcelain, and metal so acceptable to the aborigines of the lands in which they traveled, that a flourishing industry was established in Venice for the manufacture of glass beads, in the early part of the 14th century, and probably before. Among these aboriginal peoples the Indians of America were no exception, for they at once recognized the value of beads as a medium through which to express their estheticism and soon developed an art which has nowhere been surpassed.

The variety of beads most commonly used as gifts and for trade was known as seed-beads, a flattened globular form ranging in size from about a sixteenth to an eighth of an inch or more in diameter. The colors are of almost unlimited range. A preference prevailed, however, for bright red, blue, yellow, green, and opaque white. Intermediate shades were acceptable, but were used sparingly in comparison with the others. Beads of clear, colorless glass, commonly known as crystal, and black beads, were also used. The seed-beads were used chiefly for covering surfaces with fanciful designs, rather than for stringing as necklaces. Larger varieties of many forms were introduced for which other uses were found. These consisted of spherical, ovoid, tubular, and various bizarre shapes and sizes; indeed they are in such great variety that only a representative selection can here be considered.

Manufacture.—A brief description of the manufacture of glass beads is given by Dillon [35] as follows:

The manufacture and export of beads have at all times formed the very backbone of the Venetian glass industry. We cannot trace this trade back

---

[35] Dillon, Edward, Glass, London, 1907.

further than the beginning of the 14th century—by means, that is, of definite documentary evidence—but by that time a fleet of galleys was yearly dispatched on the one hand to the Black Sea, on the other to Flanders and the Thames; beads forming an important element in the cargo.

The starting point in the manufacture of beads is a rod or cane of glass: according as this cane is hollow or solid, the manufacture is carried on by radically distinct methods.

In the case of the hollow cane or tube, we start from a " gathering " at the end of the blowing iron: this gathering is slightly inflated to form a hollow pear shaped vesicle, and a rod of iron is attached to the further extremity. This rod is seized by a boy who runs with it at full speed so as to elongate the glass as much as possible before it has time to cool; the thin tube, thus formed, may, it is said, be as much as 150 feet in length. This tube, broken into sections of convenient length, are now sorted as to size by women and then are cut into shorter lengths forming bugles or tubular beads.

Spherical and barrel shaped beads are made from a solid rod of glass. The extremity of the rod is melted in a blow flame and a thread of the viscid glass is laid over a revolving iron bar. The motion of the bar draws the glass around it until the bead has assumed the desired dimensions. The size of the perforation conforms to the diameter of the iron bar. Numerous materials are used for coloring the glass before it is made into tubes or rods.

Varieties.—One kind of bead which found its way into America through early traders may be classed among the aristocrats of beads (Pl. XVIII). It has sometimes been called the "star bead," but is known among manufacturers as the " chevron bead." Many specimens of this type have been found in graves as well as in possession of living Indians, but not by any means so abundantly as other kinds, perhaps because of the greater cost of manufacture, and correspondingly lesser use. The distribution of the star beads is by no means confined to North America, where they have ranged from Florida to Canada and from coast to coast, but they found their way into many widely separated parts of Europe and into northern Africa.[36] Evidently they were distributed throughout parts of the Old World at an early period.

Among a few glass trade beads found during the excavation of the ruins at Hawikuh, New Mexico, by the Hendricks-Hodge expedition for the Museum, are two star beads, one of them differing slightly in form from those usually found in the United States and more

---

[36] Haldeman, S. S., On a Polychrome Bead from Florida, *Smithsonian Rep. for 1877,* p. 302, Washington, 1878.

nearly resembling some of the older kinds found in Europe. The larger one is spherical, a quarter of an inch in diameter, banded lengthwise with alternating lines of green, blue, and white. Around the perforations the typical star pattern in white, green, and red waves is emphasized by abrasion due to wearing on a string with other beads.[37] The smaller specimen, though only an eighth of an inch in diameter, has all the markings of the typical star bead shown in our illustration. As we have seen, it was the common custom of the early Spaniards to take beads and other trinkets as a part of their expeditionary equipment as gifts to the natives, hence it is not unlikely that the first beads were introduced among the Pueblo Indians of New Mexico and Arizona by Coronado in 1540, if not by Fray Marcos de Niza in 1539. Several other Spanish accounts of the 16th century mention the gift of beads and other trinkets to Indians.

A specimen of an unusual type of star bead was found at Point Albino, Ontario. It is globular in form; the outer surface is dark-blue, while the star pattern is produced by six alternating layers of white and green glass without the usual red band. According to Dillon [38] they belong to the hollow-tube class. His description of the structure of the bead is as follows:

The arrangement and succession of colors in the glass is in every case practically identical. The canes from which they were formed have been built up of three main concentric layers, externally a deep cobalt blue, then an opaque brick red, and in the centre a tube of pale green transparent glass; these main layers are divided by thinner ones of opaque white glass, and the dividing surfaces have been worked into a series of chevrons or zigzag (these chevrons are in all cases, I think, twelve in number) so as to present a star-like pattern on a cross section. The only variations on this general type are as follows: the chevrons are in a few cases dragged laterally so as to resemble the teeth of a circular saw; the central tube of transparent glass is sometimes divided by a zigzag layer of opaque white, and, very rarely the external layer is green instead of blue. In shape and size, however, these chevron beads show wide divergences; in length, they may vary from two and a half inches to as small as a third of an inch, and the diameter, though generally less, is in a few cases greater than the length. The extremities in some of the larger and presumably older specimens are facetted, that is to say, ground down to a pyramidal form. They

---

[37] I am informed by Mr. Hodge that these star beads formed a part of a necklace composed of almost every variety of beads used by the Zuñi inhabitants of Hawikuh.

[38] Dillon, op. cit.

were made at Murano, near Venice, the local tradition affirms, from time without memory.

A brief description of one method employed in finishing globular glass beads is found in the following quotation from Sauzay: [39]

The tubes of a diameter proportioned to that of the beads which are required, are first cut into cylinders of a height equal to their diameter, and are then placed in a pear-shaped drum of beaten iron containing a mixture of plaster and plumbago or of charcoal dust mixed with clay. The drum being placed on a furnace, the workman gives it a continuous rotatory movement by means of an iron axle which passes through it, so that the tubes softened by the heat lose the salient parts of their extremities from the constant friction with each other, and take a spherical form.

The office of the plaster and charcoal in the work is to prevent the tubes at the time of the softening of the glass, from adhering together.

A short account of the first glass-bead factory in America is given by Barber: [40]

The first industrial enterprise established in the territory of the United States was a glass bottle factory, which was erected in the Virginian colony soon after 1607. The works stood about a mile distant from Jamestown. A second glass house was erected in 1622 for the manufacture of glass beads for trade with the Indians.

Nothing is known of the exact nature of these products nor of the ultimate success of the somewhat ambitious undertaking.

Three specimens of hand-made beads of an old type and of very crude workmanship were found on St. Eustatius island in the Lesser Antilles, where they were probably introduced by early Spanish voyagers, possibly Columbus himself. These beads (fig. 81) are pentagonal and are made of two shades of blue glass.

Among the many odd forms of imported beads is one found about 1880 at Canadasaga, an old Seneca village-site near Geneva, Ontario county, New York.

FIG. 81.—Blue glass beads from St. Eustatius island, West Indies. Actual size. (10/5201).

It is of blue glass, discoidal in shape, with a lateral perforation (fig.

[39] Sauzay, A., Wonders of Glass-Making in all Ages, p. 205, New York, 1872.

[40] Barber, Edwin Atlee, American Glassware, 1900.

82). Designs in white glass have been fused on both sides. It has been said that in all probability such beads were made by Venetians for trade among the Moors and that the designs have reference to Moorish traditions. Few of these beads evidently found their way to the American Indians, and aside from the probability that their form and design pleased the natives' fancy, it is not likely that they were regarded as of any other value.

A number of glass beads made to imitate dried kernels of yellow corn (fig. 83) were found with a burial during the excavation of a Munsee cemetery near Montague, New Jersey, in 1914.[41] There are

varieties in shape and size just as one would expect to find in a handful of corn. No beads exactly like these have been found elsewhere, but a string of beads which may have been made to represent kernels of red corn has recently been collected from the Crow Indians of Montana. These, however, are not such a good imitation as the corn beads from the old Munsee cemetery.

The scarcity of such beads as those which imitate

FIG. 82.—Glass beads, probably made for Moorish trade. Ontario county, New York. Actual size. (10/4204).

FIG. 83.—Yellow glass beads made to represent grains of corn. New Jersey. Actual size. (3/7097).

yellow corn may be due to the fact that as each was separately made they did not prove profitable for trade purposes.

Mr. Louis Rosenberg, well known as a bead importer and manufacturer of New York, expresses the opinion that these yellow corn-beads were made in Venice during an early period of the bead trade with this country, while the red beads " were made sixty or seventy-five years ago in Bohemia for export to India, Africa, and America. At the time they were made there was no natural color coral glass manufactured, so they were made in crystal and covered with coral lacquer. In later years they have been made of coral and other colored glass."

---

[41] Heye, G. G., and Pepper, G. H., Exploration of a Munsee Cemetery near Montague, New Jersey, *Contr. Mus. Amer. Ind., Heye Found.,* vol. II, no. 1, 1915.

Other beads of this general class were made to represent rasp-berries, although not so perfectly as those imitating corn. Another bead takes the form of a gooseberry. Both these examples are made of clear glass, without an attempt to imitate color. The gooseberry, however, has some white lines pressed in the glass, perhaps to indi-cate the ribs in the fruit.

A distinctive type of bead of Venetian origin, known to the trade as " Cornaline d'Aleppo," is found widely distributed throughout the North American continent. These were favorably received by the Indians through the Hudson's Bay Company's trading posts, and in regions covered by the Company became known as " Hudson's Bay beads." According to an official of the Company it was one of the earliest kinds of beads used in the Canadian trade. Independent traders, no doubt, created a demand for this variety of bead in their respective regions to the southward. It has also been found in sev-eral parts of the Old World.[42] The Hudson's Bay Company's im-portations of recent years comprise seed-beads from Venice, metal and seed-beads from France, and agate beads from Bavaria.

In shape the early glass beads found with burials and at village-sites are short tubular and oblate spheroidal, and vary in length from about an eighth to a quarter of an inch. They are made in two dis-tinct colors of glass, one inside the other. The outer is always opaque red, closely resembling that commonly known as Indian red. The inner section, which is exposed at the ends, is transparent and has the appearance of being black, but by transmitted light it is usually greenish.

A more recent variety of the same general kind has yellow and white centers of opaque glass, and outside coverings of red trans-parent glass. These later beads are tubular, ovate, and spherical, and have a wide range of sizes. Some of the tubular and ovate beads are an inch or more in length, and some of the spherical ones exceed half an inch in diameter. These later beads seem to be confined to the Northwestern trade.

Trade Values.—Trade beads occurred in a wide variety of shapes, colors, and sizes, and in early days had definite values established by the Hudson's Bay Company in the North, but of these there are only a few meager records. Other traders no doubt had their standards of value, but information respecting them is negligible.

---

[42] Haldeman, S. S., On a Polychrome Bead from Florida, *Smithsonian Report for 1877*, Washington, 1878.

The standard of value recognized by the Hudson's Bay Company for general trade with the natives of their region was "one made beaver," equivalent to fifty cents, hence if an Indian desired a certain article in the trader's store, its purchase price was stated in terms of a beaver-skin or skins. The term "made beaver" is applied to a skin which has been dried and made ready for shipment to a tannery through the trader.

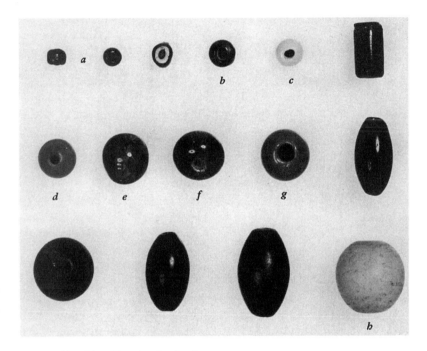

FIG. 84.—Glass beads distributed by early traders in the West. Diameter of *g,* one-half inch.

An interesting list of comparative values given in an anonymous document of the middle of the 18th century [43] includes the following:

Beads valued, one pound as one beaver, kettles, one, as one and half beaver. Powder, one pound as one beaver. Tobacco, three quarters of a pound as one beaver.

The trade values for a small variety of beads, using the term "made beaver" as the standard, was obtained at Fort McPherson on Peel river in the Canadian Northwest (fig. 84). The two beads marked

[43] A Short Statement of the Countries and Trade of North America Claimed by the Hudson's Bay Company, London, 1749.

a, of the type known to manufacturers as " Cornaline d'Aleppo " (see page 100) and to traders of the North as " Hudson's Bay beads," have an exchange value of six beads for one made beaver. A transparent green glass bead (*b*) and one of opaque yellow glass (*c*) were of the same value. A light-blue bead (*d*) had a value of three for a skin, and three others (*e–g*) two for a skin. Bead *f* is transparent amber in color; *e* and *g* are blue transparent and blue opaque respectively. Specimen *h,* a large bead of opaque glass, pale-blue in color, was the most expensive in this group, as the trader exacted two skins.

These valuations would seem rather exorbitant, but the transportation to many of the almost inaccessible trading-posts, both for the beads going in and the skins coming out, alone was a matter of consideration. The values noted are those of one trading-post only; others nearby may have had about the same value attached to other beads of the same types. Prices, however, varied in different localities. The smaller beads, known as seed-beads, are sold in " bunches " of five or six strings, each four to six inches long, according to the size and kind of beads, and having a weight of four or five bunches to the pound. The value of one bunch of seed-beads at Fort McPherson is said to be one beaver. The value of beads outside of the fur-trade of the North is not so definitely established, so far as it is possible to obtain information.

Mr. A. H. Verrill has given some information as to the value of seed-beads among the Indians of British Guiana, where a hammock is the standard of value. He states that a hammock will purchase enough beads to make a woman's apron (see fig. 99). A large apron might contain a pound of beads. A hammock would also purchase ten flasks of powder, a gun, or a girl.

Polychrome Glass Beads.—Pl. XIX illustrates a selection of polychrome glass beads from a number brought together from various localities in the West. According to the Museum collections by far the greatest number of such beads have been used by the Crows of Montana. Many indeed have been used by these Indians as offerings to the spirits of their sacred bundles, hunting charms, and similar objects. Several hundred were collected a few years ago in Morrow county, Oregon. Many of them, no doubt, had passed through the hands of nearby tribes of that locality, the Umatilla, Cayuse, and Wallawalla.

The Museum collections contain a few ornamented objects from the Blackfeet Indians, attached to which are some polychrome glass beads. A few have been procured from the Comanche, who may have acquired them through barter with tribes to the north. A string of about seventy beads was collected from a Sioux, which in all probability were obtained by barter with tribes to the north and west, rather than through a local trader. Beads of this class, all of Venetian make, have not had such wide distribution as the seed-beads, probably on account of their greater cost. They are found sparingly east of Montana. In addition to the beads shown in the illustration, which are good examples of their class, there are many others of the same type but with varying ornamentation, too numerous indeed to reproduce. Such beads were not made in a factory according to set designs, but were fashioned by families in their homes, which in a measure accounts for the great range in shape and in decorative patterns.

Funnel Beads.—Fig. 85 represents a unique form of glass bead of Venetian origin known as the " funnel bead," which is said to have been made in early days for Spanish trade in America. The term " funnel " has to do only with the outer shape. They are of two

Fig. 85.—Glass " funnel bead " from Ontario county, New York. Actual size. (13/6454).

Fig. 86.—Bead made of twisted spun glass. Tlingit. A c t u a l size. (13/8398).

kinds of glass. The upper part of the specimen illustrated is of two shades of transparent amber color, twisted spirally into shape; the lower portion is of translucent white glass. The perforation is a small parallel opening from end to end. These beads were of several colors. Our specimens are about three-quarters of an inch long. According to Mr. Rosenberg, an authority on the subject, they were not satisfactory from the standpoint of durability. The upper part, for some reason, did not fuse very solidly either in the spiral twisting or to the white glass at the base, hence the beads were easily fractured. Perhaps for this reason they did not become popular. The only specimens of this type, so far as we know, were found in Ontario county, New York—a long way from the territory traversed by early Spanish explorers.

In early days many long tubular beads were distributed throughout the country; these are in a variety of colors and sizes, and all are of opaque glass. Some of those in the Museum collection, found with burials in Cayuga county, New York, are red, evidently made to imitate the catlinite which had been used for beadmaking. Some of these beads are nearly four inches long and an eighth of an inch in diameter. Others, of blue glass and having a diameter of an eighth to a quarter of an inch, were found in Peru. Still others, of white glass, are attributed to Casas Grandes, Chihuahua, Mexico, but it is obvious that they are not from the ancient ruins of that name. These beads are not very numerous in comparison with other varieties.

Sinew-like Beads.—A necklace obtained from the Tlingit of southern Alaska includes a number of beads of unusual character. Although appearing as if made from a spirally wrapped cord of closely twisted sinew (fig. 86), they are formed of spun glass twisted into a cord and wrapped around an inner core of similar material. The cord contains glass of two colors—a single thread of pale ruby and several threads with a suggestion of yellowish brown in the twisting. The combination produces a striking resemblance to sinew. These beads were probably made at an early date in Venice, but for some reason did not attain popularity among the Indians.

WOVEN BEADWORK

Long-standing knowledge of the principle of weaving possessed by aboriginal Americans may in a great measure be attributed to the development of the many intricate methods employed in the use of beads, other than by sewing them to a surface or stringing them as necklaces. Some of the most elaborate examples of beadwork have been produced in a woven technique of one form or another. The accuracy of the mechanical part of the work, together with the artistic designs and choice of colors, is unsurpassed. In the following description of the weaving techniques, the manipulation of threads and beads has been traced by examination and analysis, in some instances by taking the work apart and rebuilding it, or by selecting a thread and following it through its sometimes baffling course. The use of beads about half an inch in diameter, with a correspondingly large string, in reproducing an intricate weave, was very helpful in solving a problem and in making the diagrams. Unfortunately, however, I have had no personal opportunity to observe the work in process by native beadworkers, and as the data on the subject have been sadly

FEATHERED BREAST-ORNAMENT DECORATED WITH SEEDS STRUNG AS BEADS AND SECTIONS OF BIRD-BONES. JIVARO INDIANS OF ECUADOR AND PERU. (13/7094) 20″ x 51″

(See inside front cover for color version.)

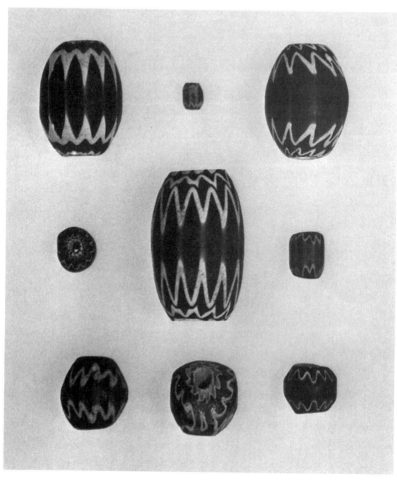

STAR OR CHEVRON BEADS FROM ONTARIO
LARGEST IS 1¾" LONG

(See inside front cover for color version.)

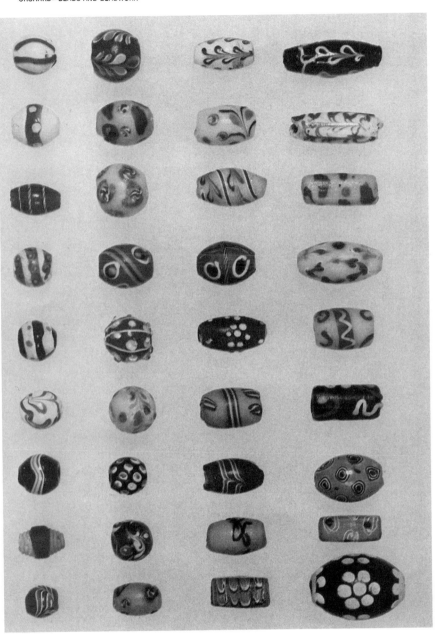

EXAMPLES OF POLYCHROME BEADS
LARGEST IS 1" LONG

(See inside back cover for color version.)

DELAWARE SHOULDER STRAP, PENNSYLVANIA   (7/5687) 19″ x 20″
(See inside back cover for color version.)

TAHLTAN LOOM WITH UNFINISHED WEAVING. (1/992)

105

neglected in the past, the material presented will lack much of interest respecting methods in general.

Square Weave

Under this heading is included that class of beadwork in which the warp and weft elements cross one another at right angles, as is understood in the ordinary method employed in weaving fabrics.

By their ingenuity the American Indians devised many ways of manipulating the threads and various kinds of looms or supports for the warp elements while the weaving progressed. With the introduction of a tastefully selected assortment of colored beads, an almost endless variety of designs was produced. A simple form of loom from the Tahltan of British Columbia, with a belt partly woven, is illustrated in Pl. XXI. The warp and weft elements are both made of threads of sinew. The warp-strands are threaded through a strip of leather, about a bead's width apart; the leather strip is reënforced with a short stick to keep it flat. The opposite ends of the warp are threaded through another strip of leather, the same width apart as before. This arrangement keeps the warp-strands parallel, and as the last-mentioned strip of leather is stiff, there is little or no danger of buckling, and reënforcement was evidently not considered necessary.

This practically constitutes what is known as a two-bar loom: that is, a bar at each end to keep the warp taut and spaced at regular intervals. In operation a leather thong or cord is tied to the reënforced end, which in turn is fastened to something rigid, such as a house timber or a stake driven into the ground. At the opposite end the warp-strands which protrude through the rawhide strip are gathered and tied with a strip of leather or cord long enough to fasten to the weaver's belt, or perhaps to go round the waist of the weaver, who, by leaning back, exerted the proper tension on the warp-strands for their convenient manipulation.

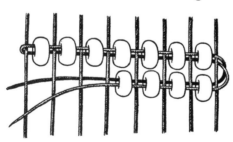

Fig. 87.—Technique of the square weave showing the use of a doubled thread for the weft. Tahltan. (1/992).

Another way of stretching such a loom has been recorded in which the weaver, in a sitting posture, attached one end to her waist while the other was looped over her foot in such a position that the tension could be regulated to meet all requirements.

Fig. 87 shows how the weft and the beads are laid across the warp. A double thread of sinew is used for the weft, which has been turned over the first warp-strand at the left of the drawing. A bead is threaded on the two strands, which are then divided and one passed over and one under the next warp element. The two weft-strands are again passed through a bead, divided, and, as before, passed one over and one under the warp. These movements are continued across the width of the weave, where a turn is made and the operation is repeated in the opposite direction. Where the turn is made the weft-threads are crossed to make the last bead secure, as shown at the right of the drawing. As the work proceeds a design is woven by inserting beads of different colors at definite intervals.

Another example of the same technique, made on fiber threads by the Astakiwi of Modoc county, California, is shown in the breast-ornament illustrated in fig. 88. The edges, however, show a different treatment: a bead has been added where the weft element turns to cross the weave (fig. 89). This places the bead with its perforation in a vertical position, while the perforations of the beads in the body of the weave are horizontal.

Fig. 88.—Breast-ornament of woven beadwork from the Astakiwi band of Achomawi in Modoc county, California. (10/9610).

Two straps for suspending the breast-ornament from the neck have been provided by tapering the weave on each edge and reducing the number of warp-strands in the middle. A width of about an inch in the middle has a finished edge, and the warp-strands are cut off at that point. On the outer edges of the straps the warp-strands (*a*) are disposed of one at a time, as the weave progresses, by catching them under the weft elements (*b*), and are then cut off. It may be noticed in the illustration (fig. 89) that the narrow straps lean toward the center of the weave, which has been accomplished by a gradual reduction of the number and length of the warp-strands in the manner that those on the outside edge were disposed of. This method of reducing or increasing the number of warp-strands in a square weave is unusual.

Another good Astakiwi example consists of a small circular basket, nine inches in diameter and two and three-quarters inches deep (fig. 90). It is of the usual Californian twine weave, and bears a design. The outer side has been covered with beads, woven to fit the curve of the basket. The technique is the same as that used in the square weave; that is, in the manner of crossing the threads, with the exception that the warp-strands are fastened directly in the center of the bottom of the basket, whence they radiate. The beads are applied spirally on a double thread, one passing under a warp, the other over. As the circle of beadwork increases, extra warp-strands become necessary and are tied to the weft or crossing strings on which the beads are threaded.

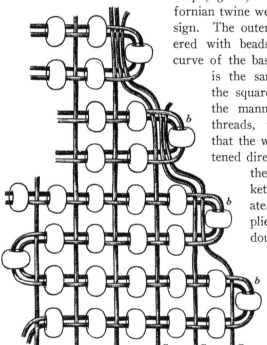

FIG. 89.—Detail of square weave showing the method of reducing the number of warp-strands. Astakiwi of Modoc county, California. (10/9610).

Most of the knots are concealed beneath the beadwork;

a few, however, show above. The weaving is attached to the basket on the bottom at the point of radiation of the warp above referred to, and at the rim along the last row of the spiral weave; otherwise it is clear of the basket. The edge, both inside and out, is covered with looped strings of beads, about half an inch in width. Although bead-

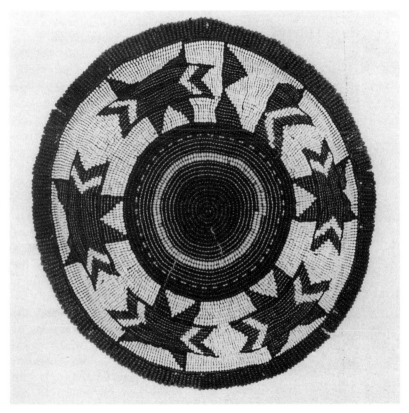

Fɪɢ. 90.—Basket covered with beadwork, woven spirally. Astakiwi of Modoc county, California. (10/9603).

work on basketry in California is common, this method is unique, and is another example of Indian ingenuity. The usual method employed in beading basketry will be described later.

Another adaptation of the square weave is shown in a child's girdle from the Patamona of the headwaters of the Mazaruni river, British

Guiana. The beads are woven around a core of threads; the warp-strands are lengthwise of the girdle; the double weft-strand carrying the beads winds around the core spirally with two beads between each pair of warp-strands. The core and the warp ends are twisted together for the strings.

Pl. XXII illustrates a portion of a wrapping for a baby carrier made by the Mono of Inyo county, California. Fashioned of red and black woolen yarn, it is fourteen and a half feet long and an inch and three-quarters wide. This is an unusual specimen of weaving, in that the beadwork is the only bonding element in the fabric. The technique is that described as the square weave with a double thread to carry the beads. A line of beads is laid across the width, with one thread above and the other below the strands of woolen yarn which form the warp, a bead between each two strands. Before another line is woven entirely across, two short rows with only four beads in each are woven in, one above the other. The remaining warp-strands are left uncovered. Then another line is woven completely across, when two more short rows are inserted as before, but on the opposite edge. This order of placing one long row and two

Fig. 91.—Finely woven shoulder bag of the Chippewa. (21/5147).

pletely across, when two more short rows are inserted as before, but on the opposite edge. This order of placing one long row and two

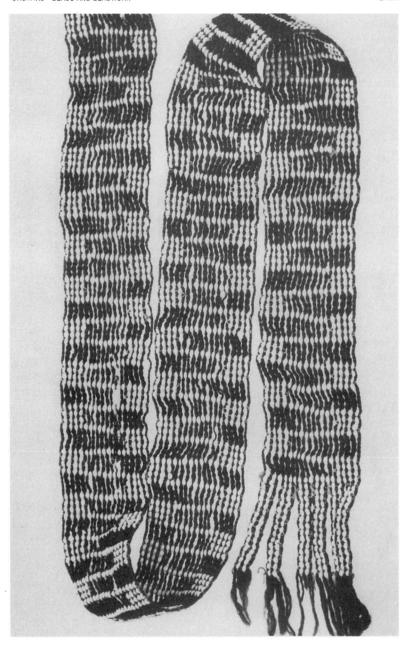

WOVEN WRAPPING FOR A BABY CARRIER. MONO OF INYO COUNTY, CALIFORNIA
(11/8748)

111

short ones is continued throughout the weave, so that the beads stand out on a dark background, making a kind of fret pattern. The background is composed of the uncovered warp elements. Despite the fact that so much of the warp is not covered or bonded in any way, the weave is firmer than might be supposed.

Another example of fine beadwork is illustrated in fig. 91, a Chippewa bag with a beaded shoulder strap.

The central panel of the bag is of woven beadwork, as are the fringe-like appendages along the lower edge. The technique of this weave is shown in fig. 92, where a single thread has been passed through the line of beads above the warp and returned through the same beads from the opposite direction and under the warp.

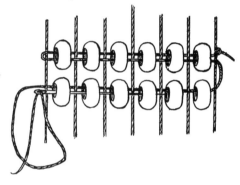

Fig. 92.—Technique of the square weave showing the use of a single thread passed through the beads from each direction.

This panel is woven separately from the bag, and afterward sewn to the cloth along the edges of the weave. The design of the panel is geometrical, and the shoulder strap has received the same treatment. The panel is bordered along the top and sides with fine-line beadwork, the sides in a net-like design, the top row of the same motive but somewhat elaborated. The coloring of the panel of the bag is very soft and is composed of fine beads, while the shoulder-strap coloring is strong

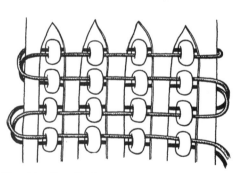

Fig. 93.—Detail of a beaded panel inserted in the fringe of an Osage pipe bag. (2/3240).

and of coarser beads, evidently not originally intended for the bag, and more than likely not made by the same person.

In this technique the warp-strands are stretched between two bars, one attached to a rigid post set in the ground or to a house-post, the other fastened by means of a cord to the weaver's belt. Another method employed is a fixed stretcher in the form of a frame on which the two bars are on opposing sides: in other words, a two-bar loom.

A pipe bag of the Osage bears a rather unusual form of decoration. In addition to the ornamentation on the body of the bag, a panel of beading is inserted on the fringe, which is of the square-weave type. The warp-strands are supplied by strands of the leather fringe. The beads are attached by the usual method of passing two threads through a bead, one thread going over and the other under the leather strip forming the warp (fig. 93). This panel is about four by four and a half inches. A design is produced by the use of beads of contrasting colors.

A specimen of similar technique was obtained from the Cheyenne.

The Heddle.—Varieties of the square weave have been produced by the Menomini, Sauk and Fox, Chippewa, Winnebago, Micmac, and nearby tribes with the aid of a heddle (fig. 94), a wooden contrivance usually rather elaborately made and decorated. It is provided with a number of equally spaced bars. One series of the warp-strands passes between the bars, another through perforations or " eyes of the heddle " in the center of the bars. These threads are in a fixed position, while those passing between the bars are free to slide up or down. When the warp is taut, one series is above the other, that is, there is a space or " shed " between the two series. In textile weaving the shed is provided for the passage of the shuttle carrying the weft or crossing thread. A vertical movement of the heddle changes the position of the threads, thus if those threads which are passing through the eyes are above, by lowering the heddle they are carried down and become the lower series, while those having freedom of movement in the spaces are above.

Following each movement of the heddle the shuttle is thrown across the weave, laying the weft between the warp-strands in the shed. If one can visualize these movements it will be seen that the fixed threads, or those passing through the eyes of the heddle, first cross over a weft, and at the next movement cross under, while the free threads first cross under and then over. This is the process of a simple over-and-under weave. The same principle applies to either a hand or a power loom.

It cannot be said that the type of heddle illustrated (fig. 94) is an invention of the Indians. It was probably introduced by the Jesuits

or early French settlers. However, the contrivance found favor, and
was used to some extent with good results. The Indian procedure is
to thread the warp-strands of necessary length through the heddle.
The ends where the beading is to be commenced are wrapped around

FIG. 94.—Wooden heddle of the Menomini. (8/4621).

and fastened to a small stick, spread to about the width desired for
the width of the weave. The opposite ends of the warp are drawn
taut and knotted, each thread having as nearly the same tension as
possible. The knotted end is fastened to a support of some kind,
perhaps a pole driven into the ground; the opposite end is fastened to
the beadworker's belt, so that, by a movement either toward or from
the pole, the warp is kept at the proper tension. Beads are strung on
the weft-strand and passed through the shed, alternating the position
of the warp between each crossing of the weft first from one side,
then the other. The beads are placed with two warp-strands between
them (fig. 95). So far the process is simple: that is, if the beads
are all of the same color, and no pattern is being woven.

The introduction of a design with no other guide than a mental
pattern is a complicated and difficult operation. In this case the
beads have to be counted and spaced on the weft according to color
as each line is added. By this method some elaborate designs of

excellent workmanship have been woven, but by no means do they excel other methods of producing the square weave which have been described.

The use of the heddle has been confined to a comparatively limited area and to the tribes already mentioned.

Bow loom.—An apron of woven beadwork constituting a woman's dress is illustrated in fig. 96. This form of garment is common

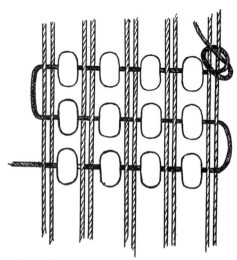

among several tribes of northern South America and in some parts of the Amazon region. The method of weaving, and the details of the bow loom used, are described from specimens and data collected in the Guianas. The loom consists of a bowed stick with a cross-piece secured at the extremities of the bow. This serves the double purpose of insuring the permanent curve of the bow and of providing a support for the warp-strands during the operation of weaving.

FIG. 95.—Detail of the arrangement of threads and beads in weaving: two threads for the warp, one thread for the weft.

The looms vary in size according to the dimensions of the apron to be made. That illustrated in fig. 96 is about twenty-two inches wide between the intersections of the cross-stick and the bow. No attempt seems to have been made to trim the sticks beyond cutting off the branches, hence it is evident that the loom is discarded when the weaving is completed. Cotton and other fibers are used for the warp and weft elements. It may be well to mention that an apron is woven upside down.

The weaving process is commenced by fastening four strings across the bow, about midway between the cross-stick and the base. These are long enough to form the tie-strings of the completed apron. Warp elements are woven into the four strings, which are twisted in pairs, with a warp-thread between each twist. As indicated in the drawing (fig. 97) the warp is looped along the upper edge; the loose ends are taken care of at the lower or finishing edge of the apron. In the illustration the cords are spread apart to show their several

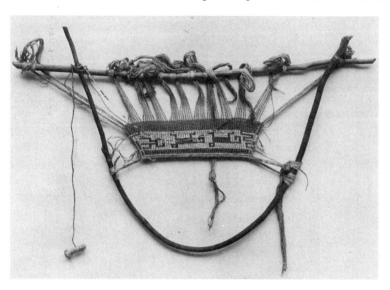

Fig. 96.—Apron loom and partly completed apron. Arekuna Indians, upper Essequibo river, British Guiana. (4/9922).

directions; when drawn together tightly they form the upper selvage edge of the apron. In the next step the warp-strands are separated into groups of about six strands each and loosely tied to the cross-bar (see fig. 96).

Fig. 97.—Upper edge of a woman's apron showing the method of placing the warp-strands through two pairs of twisting strings. These strings would be inverted on the loom. (4/9922).

The manufacture of a bead apron is woman's work, and the loom is now ready to receive the beads. With her legs through the loop of the bow, either sitting on the ground or in some other convenient position (fig. 98), the woman doubles a thread around the first warp element at her right-hand side, then proceeds to thread beads on the doubled thread in number sufficient to complete the first row, which

Fig. 98.—Patamona woman weaving a bead apron on a bow-loom.

is usually of one color. Sometimes two rows are of one color. The first group of warp-strands is untied from the cross-bar, and each strand in its order is passed through the doubled string of beads, one warp element between two beads. The group of warp-strands are then tied in place and the next group treated in the same manner. This is an unusual movement in weaving, the common method being to cross the weft-thread under and over a permanently fixed warp. The reason the warp has been tied in groups to the cross-bar is that they are out of the way when not being used, and are easily untied as occasion demands. On the completion of a line across the apron, the loom is turned around so that the beading may always proceed from right to left. Should the next row of beads be selected for the starting of a design, the beads are strung as before, but are sorted in colors by count as they are to appear in the pattern, each row being so treated. The process of passing the warp element through the weft or beaded string is the same throughout the weaving of the apron. At the end of each line of beading two of the warp-strands are twisted once around so that they shall hold the weft in place as it is crowded down on to the row beneath. It will be noticed in the illustration that the width of the apron increases as the beading proceeds, necessitating the use of more warp-strands in proportion; these are added by tying an extra pair on the sides as needed.

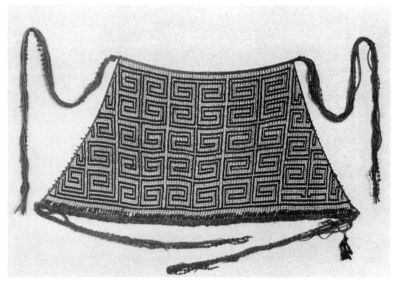

FIG. 99.—Apron of a Makusi woman of Ireng river, British Guiana. Width at bottom, 17 in. (7/4908).

The incomplete apron shown in fig. 96 has at each side an edging composed of two doubled warp-strands, each of which has been twisted over the weft, the usual treatment as before described for the extreme edge. These two elements are separated by two beads, producing an additional ornamentation to the finished apron in contrast to the plain single edging to the complete apron shown in fig. 99.

A supply of extra warp-strands is kept near at hand, usually tied in a bunch to one side of the bow. At the completion of the weave the ends of the warp-threads are beaded in the form of a fringe.

The tribes represented by the Museum collection of this type of beadwork are the Arekuna, Waika, Akawai, Patamona, Atorai, Wapishana, and Makusi. Further exploration may supply knowledge of a much wider distribution of this form of apron.

Variations of the Square Weave.—A pair of garters from the Winnebago shows a rather unusual variation of the square weave, in which only a single thread is used for the weft and warp elements, except the edges, which are reënforced with a double thread. The

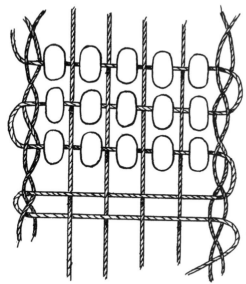

weft crosses over and under the warp (fig. 100), with a bead between each crossing, the usual square-weave method, but does not pass through the same beads a second time when going in the opposite direction, as in the previous single-thread weft technique described; instead, it is carried on to the next row of beads. As the drawing shows, the double warp at the edges is twisted between and under each turn of the crossing thread. The threads are made of wool

Fig. 100.—Single-thread warp and weft. Winnebago. (9002).

yarn. At the finished ends, the warp-strands are grouped together and braided for tie-strings.

Included in the contents of an old war bundle of the Sauk of Oklahoma was a pair of woven beaded garters (fig. 101), no doubt a part of the paraphernalia worn during ceremonies connected with the bundle. They are of the square weave, that is, the warp and weft elements cross one another at right angles. The threads are all made of spun buffalo-wool, twisted into two-ply cords, the warp about twice the size of the weft. A single strand is used for the weft and two strands for the warp. The weave (fig. 102) is bonded by two warp-strands being twisted one over the other between the rows of beads, the weft passing through the twists. The weft is a continuous thread, crossing from one side of the weave to the other, making a loop at each turn through which the warp-strands are twisted. The drawing, though only three beads wide, is sufficient to show the movement of the weaving elements. The beaded area in these two garters is eleven by two and a quarter inches in each specimen. At each end the warp-strands are secured by about three-quarters of an inch of weaving without the insertion of beads; the remaining loose ends are left as a fringe. The beads are blue and white, known as "pony beads," a term derived from the fact that "pony traders," or traveling traders with pack-animals, were said to have introduced that variety. The beads are larger than those generally used, being about an eighth of an inch or more in diameter, whereas the more common variety is about half that size.

There is every indication that this technique is an old style of Indian weave which was in use to some extent soon after the introduction of beads. The knowledge of twined weaving in basketry may have been responsible for the use of this method in weaving such soft fabrics as are herein described. A number of specimens in the Museum collections, undoubtedly made at an early period, are so woven. The threads are made of ravelings from woolen cloth which was distributed among the natives in early days. Later, commercial

Fig. 101.—Beaded garters of the Sauk. (2/8738).

threads were introduced and evidently became popular, perhaps because they were regarded as a labor-saving commodity, if not as a
novelty. With the use of threads instead of cloth ravelings, the
twined or twisted weave was apparently abandoned in favor of the

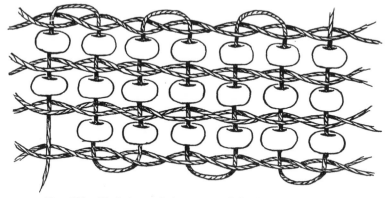

Fig. 102.—Technique of the weave of Sauk beaded garters.

more simple square weave, in which two weft-strands are made to
pass over one warp-strand, with a bead between the warp-strands
holding the weft-strands together.

Specimens of the twined-warp weave have been collected from the
Mohegan, Narragansett, Alibamu, Koasati, Seminole, Osage, Sauk,
Menomini, Shawnee, and Winnebago Indians.

A simple form of the square weave was employed in assembling
wampum beads for use as belts. The warp-strands consisted either
of leather thongs (which in the Museum collections predominate) or
of cords made of vegetal fiber. The weft elements consist of vegetal
fiber, or very rarely of sinew threads. Descriptions of the processes
as recorded by early observers are very indefinite. An account of
comparatively recent date was written by Lewis H. Morgan,[44] for
whom a belt was made at Tonawanda, New York, in 1850. There
is every reason to believe that both the loom and the process of weaving correspond with methods and devices of an earlier period. The
loom described by Morgan is known as the bow-loom, but one is
hardly justified in assuming that this was employed exclusively, for
other means of stretching the warp elements, or lengthwise strings,
have been mentioned, although so vaguely that there are insufficient
data to reconstruct such a device. Morgan's account follows:

[44] Morgan, Lewis H., League of the Ho-de'-no-sau-nee, or Iroquois, Lloyd
ed., vol. II, pp. 54–55, New York, 1904.

In belt-making, which is a simple process, eight strands of cords or bark thread are first twisted from filaments of slippery elm, of the requisite length and size; after which they are passed through a strip of deerskin to separate them at equal distances from each other in parallel lines. A

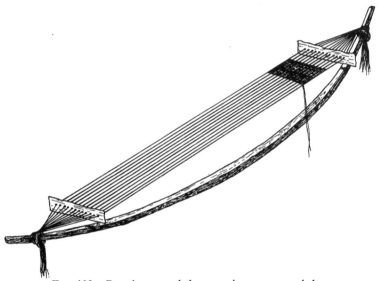

Fig. 103.—Bow-loom used for weaving wampum belts.

splint is then sprung in the form of a bow, to which each end of the several strings is secured, and by which all of them are held in tension, like warp threads in a weaving machine. Seven beads, these making the intended width of the belts, are then run upon a thread by means of a needle, and are passed under the cords at right angles, so as to bring one bead lengthwise between each cord and the one next in position. The thread is then passed back along the upper side of the cords, and again through each of the beads; so that each bead is held firmly in its place by means of two threads, one passing under and one above the cords. This process is continued until the belt reaches its intended length, when the ends of the cords are tied, the end of the belt covered and afterwards trimmed with ribbons. In ancient times both the cords and thread were of sinew.

We thus have a clear idea of the manner in which wampum belts were woven, a process which may be said to have been applied in making all such belts, with perhaps a few minor exceptions. For example, many of the existing belts are woven on leather thongs, and vegetal fibers are known to have been used for cords and strings, such as dogbane (*Apocynum cannabinum*), sometimes called armyroot and black Indian hemp; swamp milkweed (*Asclepias incarnata*), and the hairy milkweed (*A. pulchra*), also called white Indian hemp; toad flax (*Linaria linaria*), and Indian mallow (*Abutilon abutilon*), also known as velvet leaf.

Fig. 103 is a drawing of a bow-loom as described by Morgan, showing the warp-strands spread apart at equal distances by being passed through perforations in pieces of leather or other suitable material, such as birch-bark.

The manner of threading the beads varied. Instead of using a single thread (fig. 104), as described by Morgan, a great majority of

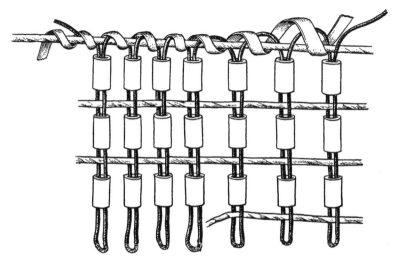

FIG. 104. Technique of single-thread weave. The weft is led across in one direction and back again through the same beads in the opposite direction. Seneca. (10/4264).

the belts reveal the use of a doubled thread as shown in fig. 105. The thread is first doubled over an outside warp-strand, as at *a* in the drawing, and the two threads are then passed through a bead. They are then separated, and one passed over and one under the next warp-strand, when another bead is threaded on the two strings, which are again separated and passed one over and one under the next warp-strand. This operation is repeated until the entire width is filled with beads, when the two strings are twisted (*b*) with one or more turns, and are made to cross the weave in the opposite direction, a bead being placed between each pair of warp-strands as in the first movement. This process is continued until the weave is complete. A design is incorporated by the insertion of purple and white beads at definite intervals. The ends of the weft or crossing strings are secured by a simple knot, when the last bead is strung, or where a new string is to be added. The ends of the warp-strands, which usually project beyond the ends of the woven portion, form a fringe at each end. Sometimes the ends are brought together and braided. A small proportion of the belts have an extra binding along the edges, consisting of a narrow strip of leather (fig. 104) wrapped around the outside warp-strands with a single turn between the rows of beads covering and concealing the crossing strings, in all probability to save wear and tear of those strings

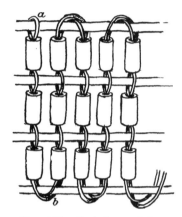

Fig. 105.—Technique of double-thread weave. The two strands are worked together.

and thereby to prevent the breaking and destruction of the belt. Apparently there was no fixed rule for the length or breadth of the belts, which varied from five or six beads in width to as many as occasion or fancy dictated. The widest belt known is mentioned by Beauchamp [45] as being fifty beads wide. The Penn wampum belts [46] in the Museum are approximately twenty-five inches long, one being fifteen, the other eighteen, beads wide, or about four and a quarter and five and a quarter inches. Another belt in the collection is sixty-six inches long.

A band of imitation wampum beads of black and white glass, woven in the manner commonly employed for wampum belts (see Pl. XXIII), has been used to ornament a headdress made of deerskin and a piece of a red blanket, further ornamented with albino buffalo-hair and horns. The strings used for weaving the beads are made from ravelings of a red blanket. This headdress, of Sauk origin, is in the Milwaukee Public Museum.

A belt made of the same kind of beads and of the usual wampum-

[45] Beauchamp, W. M., Wampum and Shell Articles Used by the New York Indians, *Bull. 41, N. Y. State Mus.*, p. 412, Albany, 1901.

[46] Speck, F. G., and Orchard, W. C., The Penn Wampum Belts, *Leaflet 4, Mus. Amer. Ind., Heye Found.*, 1925.

SAUK HEADDRESS ORNAMENTED WITH IMITATION WAMPUM
(Courtesy of the Milwaukee Public Museum)

125

belt weave came to the Museum of the American Indian with an interesting history. It is said to have been taken by Gen. Benjamin Bellows, of New Hampshire, in personal combat with an Indian during the Revolution, and is probably of Micmac origin. It is four feet long and four inches wide. This specimen and the headdress above mentioned indicate that imitation wampum was introduced at an early date; but it did not become popular, perhaps because the color bore no resemblance to shell wampum. A few glass-wampum beads have appeared from time to time; these have been made to look somewhat like the well-known purple shell beads, but the imitation is so poor that, if their scarcity is an indication, they also were not received with favor by the Indians.

A rather complicated weave in the form of neckbands has come to the Museum from the Guaymi Indians of central Chiriqui, Panama. The general appearance closely resembles that which we have described as the square weave, produced in quantities by the Indians of northern United States and Canada. An analysis, however, reveals a method of assembling beads entirely different from any employed by northern beadworkers. The neckbands vary in width from about seven-eighths of an inch to two inches and in length from ten to fourteen inches, exclusive of the tie-strings, which are the ends of the warp-strands.

The weave is shown in detail in fig. 106, a few beads in width, sufficient to show the movement of the weaving elements. At the upper right-hand corner of the drawing a solid black line representing a thread (a) may be traced by dotted lines through the top row of beads to the left extremity, where it turns down and passes through the first bead of the row immediately beneath, then through the second bead of the third row, the third bead of the fourth row, and so on diagonally across the weave until it reaches the outer edge where at d it is turned directly across the weave again. When it reaches the opposite side the diagonal crossing is repeated.

The thread marked b, represented by a double line in the drawing, is shown to pass through the first bead from left to right, then to the line below, and straight across, where it makes a downward turn and crosses diagonally in the same manner as the first thread. The twisted string c passes through the second bead of the top row, and the first of the second row, in both cases from left to right, then through the first of the third row from right to left, and straight across, following with the diagonal crossing as did the two previous strings. These three threads are given different markings so that they may be easily traced in their movements throughout the weave. The succeeding strings follow the same courses.

In producing this weave the beads of the first row are strung on the crossing thread *a,* in number according to the determined width of the object; then the other strings are added in order, *b, c,* etc. The second row is then threaded on the second string, and the following threads passed through in their proper order. After the first two rows are completed the rest of the operation is comparatively easy and is carried through in the same manner line for line. The long ends of the threads above the first row are gathered into groups of three or four, and a number of beads threaded on each group. These threads are so arranged at each end of the weave and are of such length as to form tie-strings for the neckband. The extreme ends are left uncovered and are braided into a single strand.

In the progress of weaving the completed part is wrapped around a small stick for convenience.

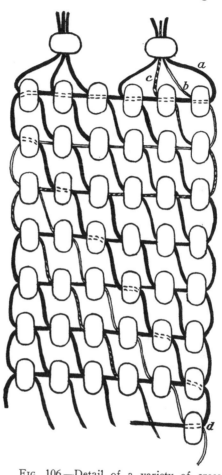

Fig. 106.—Detail of a variety of cross-weaving by the Guaymi Indians of Panama. (13/7616).

The beadworker carries his supply of beads, strung in assorted colors, in a small gourd attached to his belt. Designs are introduced by inserting beads of different colors at counted intervals, without the aid of a pattern. The work is done by the men of the tribe in their spare moments, much as our women do their knitting, taking their work with them while visiting their neighbors or to occupy their time when traveling. Beads of the most brilliant colors are evidently preferred; the softer shades in the examples of beadwork of the northern Indians are entirely lacking. Gaudy glass beads made to imitate burnished gold and silver are popular with many of the Panama people. A number of ornaments made of these have been added to the Museum's collections.

Another interesting variety of the square weave was found among the Mosquito Indians of Nicaragua. Fig. 107 shows the movement of the threads employed. That marked *a* is a continuous weft-thread passing through the rows of beads first from right to left, then turning down to the next row and going from left to right, on again to the next from right to left, and so on throughout the weave. The warp-strands *c* and *d* are added from the right side of the beads along the top row, then alternate with each row. Threads *b* and *e* are started from left to right to insure the correct disposal of loops along the edge. As the drawing shows, only every other bead is supplied with a warp element. The objects so made are in the form of neckbands which vary in width from an inch to two niches and in length from ten to fourteen inches. The warp-strands are made sufficiently long to form the tie-strings gathered into groups, partly beaded and braided into a unit.

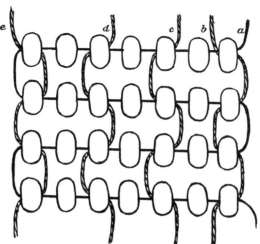

Fig. 107.—Detail of the "skip weave" in neckbands from Nicaragua. (13/2553).

BIAS WEAVE

An example of weaving in which the warp and weft elements change places in alternating lines, the warp becoming the weft and the weft taking the place of the warp, is illustrated in fig. 108. The

specimen was made for a neckband, of dark
blue and white beads, with horsehair for warp
and weft elements. The stiff unwieldy nature of the horsehair does not produce a soft,
pliable weave, for which reason, perhaps, articles so constructed are not by any means
common. The procedure in this case was to
select hairs long enough to obviate the neces-
sity of introducing new ones, so far as possible. The extreme length of the specimen
illustrated is fourteen inches, and only close
examination reveals where a few new hairs
have been added. The same weave, but with
soft fiber instead of horsehair, has been
largely used for streamers on hair-ornaments,
also for necklaces by several tribes, but it
does not appear to have had a wide distribution. The tribes represented by the Museum's
collection are the Prairie and Forest Potawa-
tomi, Menomini, Sauk, Fox, Delaware, Oto,
and Winnebago. Dr. Speck collected specimens woven on horsehair from the Osage.[47]

From the East we have an example of the
weave on soft fiber from the Penobscot in
Maine, said to have been in the possession of
one family since 1825. In this case, however,
the beads are purple wampum with an edging of white wampum. The object is in the
form of a band, thirty inches long by an inch
and a half wide, and was used as a neck- or
breast-ornament. An interesting feature of
this specimen is that the beading is so arranged as to produce a curve to the band
(fig. 109), this result having been brought
about by inserting beads of graded lengths
at the points where the ornament leaves the
shoulders to cross the breast. The shortest

Fig. 108.—Neckband
of bias weave with
horsehair warp- and
weft-strands. Fox In-
dians. (2/7849).

[47] Speck, F. G., Ethnology of the Yuchi Indians,
University of Pennsylvania Museum, Anthr. Publ.,
vol. I, no. 1, p. 49, Philadelphia, 1909.

beads are woven into the upper edge, and gradually longer ones are used as the lower edge is approached; consequently the lower edge is expanded and the upper contracted so far as the graded beads have been used.

There are three such specimens in the Museum collections from the Penobscot. Long streamers of this weave on soft fiber were worn by

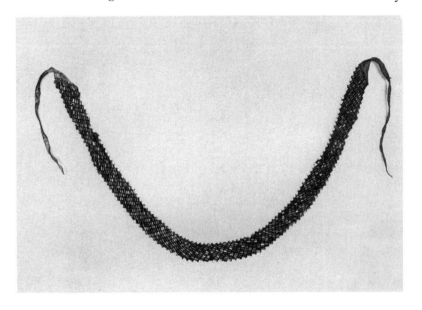

Fig. 109.—Wampum necklace of bias weave. Penobscot. (8182).

women of Western tribes mentioned above, attached to the hair at the back. The hair was gathered and drawn tightly from front to back, parted at the middle, and then enclosed in a piece of cloth about five inches wide and fifteen inches long, usually wrapped with a woven bead-strip of square weave, not the bias weave, and quite frequently with some highly esteemed silk ribbon of brilliant color. The cloth wrapping was invariably ornamented with panels of beading at each end, sewed directly to the cloth. The streamers only were of the bias weave, of width varying from a quarter of an inch to an inch and a quarter, and about four feet long.

The same technique was employed for the horsehair and soft fiber weaving. The detail of the weave is shown in fig. 110. The weaving elements are in pairs, knotted through a strip of soft-tanned leather about a bead-width apart. A bead is threaded on the first pair, which we will call the warp, at the right-hand side when they are separated, one strand being passed over and one under the next or second pair, when another bead is threaded, the strands separated,

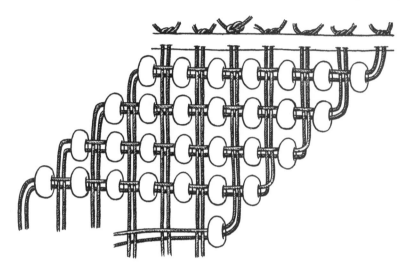

FIG. 110.—Detail of the bias weave. Fox Indians. (2/7849).

and passed over and under in the same manner. The movement is repeated until the row is completed, when the two strands are turned down lengthwise. During this movement the strands are used as a weft element, and in turning them down they become the warp. The second pair at the right are treated as were the first, and so with the succeeding strands, until the weave is finished. The ends of the horsehairs or threads of other material are then passed through a piece of soft-tanned leather and knotted as in the beginning, when the edges of the leather are sewed together, which conceals the knotted ends. The leather strip is about half an inch wide and long enough to make tie-strings when the article is to be used as a neckband.

Many elaborate designs have been wrought in this weave by the use of various colored beads. These designs are mostly geometric, although some attempt has been made to depict flowers and leaves, and one specimen bears a design representing birds.

Under the head of streamers there is an interesting method of manufacture which consists of a simple three-strand braid with a bead inserted at each outside turn of the braiding. The detail is shown in fig. 111.

A variation of the bias weave occurs in some neck-ornaments collected from the Chippewa of Minnesota. The method hitherto described is that by which the beads are threaded on the crossing or horizontal strings; but in this variation the beads are on the vertical

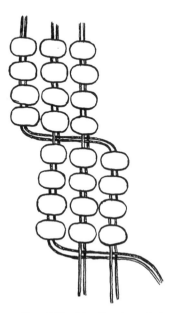

Fig. 111.—Detail of three-strand braid streamer. Kickapoo. (10/5615).

Fig. 112.—Detail of variation in bias weave. The beads are strung on the vertical threads. Chippewa. (10/1288).

threads, which are in pairs. When they are turned to cross the weave, they are passed between the upright strings. The drawing (fig. 112) indicates the use of four beads to a string, sufficient to show the variation in technique, whereas the specimens have seven or eight beads on each pair of strings, and are eight strings in width.

Pl. XXIV illustrates a common form of a diagonally woven sash ornamented with white beads inserted during the weaving, and the accompanying sketch (fig. 113) shows how the thread bearing the beads is incorporated into the weave. The beads are strung on a small thread, not the woolen yarn of which the sash is made. The thread is woven in between the weaving elements, crossing over and under in regular order with a bead between each crossing. This technique limits the introduction of designs other than angular pat-

PART OF AN IROQUOIS SASH WITH WHITE BEADS INTERWOVEN
THE DARK PORTION IS OF RED WORSTED; THE EDGES ARE GRAY. (2/9675)

terns which follow the course of the weaving strands.   This form of ornamentation is widely distributed, and is common among some of the Iroquois tribes.   The Kickapoo, Menomini, Sauk, Fox, Chippewa, Creek, Osage, Micmac, and Ponca have contributed this technique to the Museum collections.

A small bag of woven beadwork, made by a Comanche Indian for holding cornhusks cut to shape for use as cigarette wrappers, reveals an interesting and somewhat complicated technique. The specimen is independent of any support for the beads other than t h e threads w o v e n through them.   According-ing to some very indefi-nite information, the bag was woven on a smooth round stick.   W h e n completed the weave was tubular in form, and was slid from the stick, one end of the tube being closed with some overlaid stitches to make a bag.

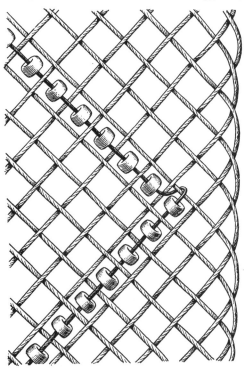

Fig. 113.—Detail of part of a beaded woven sash. The bead-bearing thread crosses over and under the warp- and weft-strands. Seneca. (9470).

In the process of making, the first row of beads is held together by means of two threads, which are passed through each bead, crossing each other in the perforation indicated by the dotted lines in fig. 114.   This forms the foundation, which is wrapped around the smooth round stick of suitable size, preferably slightly tapering.   The succeeding rows of beads are built up spirally on the foundation by a thread passing down through a bead, through a connecting loop of the foundation string, up through the same bead again, and on to the next bead.   The illustration shows the movement of the threads.   The specimen is ornamented with various colored beads so arranged as to make a wave-like design, with ex-cellent results.

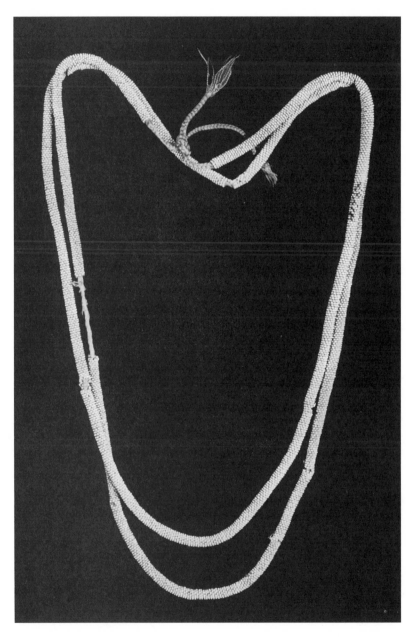

NECKLACE OF SMALL GLASS BEADS FROM GUATEMALA. ACTUAL SIZE. (5/6592)

The same technique has been used with very small beads (Pl.
XXV) in making a necklace from Guatemala; but unfortunately it is

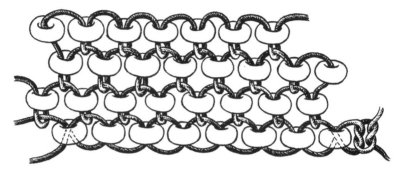

FIG. 114.—Detail of the weave of a Comanche bag for cigarette wrappers of
cornhusk. (5/6592).

without definite data, and indeed it is not positively known to be of
Indian origin. The interesting features of the object are that this

FIG. 115.—Chipped blades with woven bead decoration.
Ute. (13/6930, 13/6931).

particular technique should be found in Guatemala, and the size of beads used. It is truly a microscopic piece of work. The beads, known to the trade as Tinised beads, are the smallest made, being only about a thirty-second of an inch in diameter.

Two specimens of woven beadwork similar in technique to the Comanche pouch and the necklace from Guatemala have been collected from the Ute, consisting re-

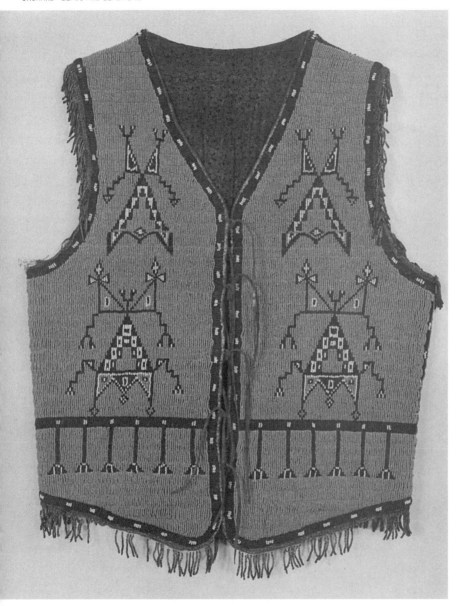

OGLALA SIOUX MAN'S VEST. (23/2540) 19″ x 24″

(See front cover for color version.)

SIOUX WOMAN'S BUCKSKIN DRESS. (20/6809) 51″ LONG

(See inside back cover for color version.)

spectively of a chipped stone knife-blade or spear-point, and a stone arrowpoint (fig. 115), decorated with colored beads bearing designs and probably made for use as charms. The parts to be decorated were first covered with cotton cloth, fitted closely to the shape of the object. The first row of beads is sewn to the edge of the cloth around the middle of each of the objects. The thread passes down through a bead into the cloth and up through the bead again, then on to the next bead (fig. 116), which is treated in the same manner, and so continued around. The succeeding rows of beads are sewn in the same way, but instead

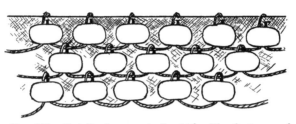

FIG. 116.—Detail of weave in fig. 115. The first row of beads is sewn to the cloth foundation.

of the thread entering the cloth, it is caught under the threads, passing from one bead to the other around the first row. The difference between these two specimens and the small Comanche pouch and Guatemala necklace is in the commencement, otherwise the technique is the same. The interesting feature is the well-formed symmetrical design produced on objects of such irregular shapes.

Parental affection for children is proverbial among the American Indians, a fact exemplified by the stupendous piece of work in ornamenting the Comanche cradle, or baby-carrier, shown in Pl. XXXXI. The frame is of wood, decorated at the points with a few brass-headed nails; the body is of tanned deerskin lined with cotton cloth. The decoration of the body consists of a solid covering of very fine glass beads; the artistic designs are wrought in various colors, while the background is of opaque white beads. There are about four hundred and thirty square inches of this beadwork, with about two hundred and eighty beads to the square inch, hence the number of beads aggregates one hundred and twenty thousand. A somewhat intricate technique has been employed, in that two threads have been passed through each bead. Taking into consideration the number of beads and stitches, and the fine calculation necessary to produce the elaborate design, one can imagine the amount of time and energy spent in this labor of love.

The technique and the relation of beads one to another in this elaborate object are shown in fig. 117. It will be seen that the combination of beads and threads forms a kind of network, with the beads taking the place of knots at the corners of the meshes. It must be

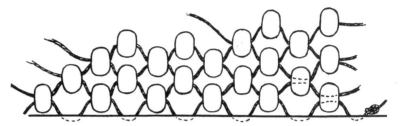

FIG. 117.—Detail of woven beadwork on the Comanche cradle shown in Pl. XXXXI. (5/7467)

understood that the drawing shows the work spread apart to illustrate clearly the direction of the threads; in the original decoration the beads are all in contact, concealing the threads. The single line across the bottom of the drawing represents the leather base to which is attached the first course of beads. This was done by sewing a row of beads in a straight line across the leather, spaced apart so that a second row may interlock. The illustration shows the way in which the first row is held in place, the dotted lines indicating where the thread has entered the leather. The second row of beads is not sewed to the leather, but to the first row by passing a thread through the beads, as shown. The succeeding rows are sewed one to another in the same way, the beads interlocking. The insertion of the design takes place as the rows of beads are laid together. The various colors are placed in the continuous lines as they are built up, requiring fine calculation as to where and how many beads are to be employed, so that the design shall be well balanced and in the proper position. Some roughly drawn pattern may have been at hand as a guide, perhaps some markings with charcoal on a piece of leather, or a pencil and paper may have been used; often, however, such work was accomplished without the aid of a pattern.

The work on this specimen was done in sections. There are three spaces without pattern where the beads are laid on in a direction opposite to that of the rest of the work. The entire mass of the weaving is fastened to the leather base only around the edges of the sections. The finishing edge is fastened in the same manner as for the first edge, as shown in the illustration; the side-threads have their ends knotted into the leather.

Among certain tribes property right in designs is recognized. Many designs are derived from dreams. Thus, if a woman or a man has a particular form suggested in a dream, it is carefully worked out and perhaps elaborated during waking hours. Should the design prove attractive to other persons, or if some potency should be attributed to it, before others may use it a price must be paid to the original owner or his consent to the use of it must be obtained.

Baby carriers, or cradles, differing in form and technique, and more or less ornamented, are widespread among the Indians. The materials of which they were made were often selected with care and ceremony. Porcupine quills, dyed in many colors, and beads were used in the decoration, particularly by the Indians of the Plains. Many fine examples are in the Museum collections.

A pair of wristlets of Comanche origin are ornamented with a bead technique similar to that used on the baby carrier shown in Pl. XXXXI. The foundation in this instance is different. The first row of beads are sewed to the leather in such a position that the perforations are vertical; the succeeding rows are secured in the same manner as in the decoration of the baby-carrier. This beadwork technique occurs to some extent among the Kiowa, Comanche, and Caddo, and it is found on costumes, including footwear, and on ceremonial objects. Many of the wands, rattles, and sashes used in the Peyote ceremony are thus decorated with elaborate designs and esthetic coloring.

NET-LIKE WEAVE

Examples of a net-like weave of beads, including several variations, have been collected from many parts of the North American continent, the same fundamental principle being applied throughout; that is, a bead is made to function as a knot in netting. Most of the specimens are neck-ornaments.

The neck-ornament shown in Pl. XXVIII was produced by the Washo of Nevada. The foundation consists of a piece of cotton cloth through which the strings of the netting are tied in pairs, as shown in detail in fig. 118. A bead is threaded on each pair of strings and placed in contact with the cotton cloth. The strings are then separated and three beads are strung on the single threads. At this stage the nearest strings of the adjoining pairs are brought together and held with one bead; then the strings are separated and each supplied with three beads. The strings forming the original pairs are then held together with one bead, separated again, and three beads strung, brought together as before, and supplied with a bead which holds the meshes together. This operation completes a series of diamond-shape meshes, as shown in the illustration. The length of the cloth

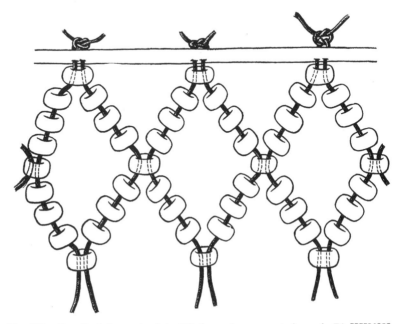

Fig. 118.—Detail of the mesh of the Washo neck-ornament shown in Pl. XXVIII. (8/4582)

foundation and the number of pairs of strings used are of course determined by the size of the object to be made. The specimen under discussion is 14¾ inches long and 8½ inches wide. The length of the meshes averages half an inch. The ends of the strings are threaded with a number of beads, forming a fringe along the lower edge of the beadwork. The strings in this weave are all vertical, and the cotton cloth which forms the foundation is long enough to provide tie-strings.

One of the variations is shown in a headband (Pl. XXIX) made by Indians of San Juan river, Columbia. The foundation, instead of being a strip of cloth as in the case of the Washo specimen (Pl. XXVIII), is a string with closely threaded beads the entire length of the object (fig. 119). The strings forming the body or network are looped

NECK ORNAMENT OF THE WASHO. (8/4582)

141

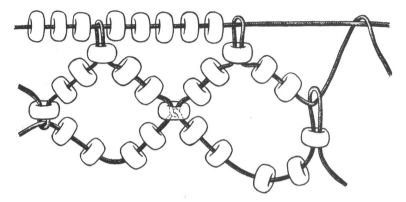

FIG. 119.—Detail of the mesh of the headband shown in Pl. XXIX. (1/2259).

along the foundation cord with four beads between each looping. In making the loop, the thread is passed up through a bead, over the foundation cord, and down through the same bead. Then two beads are strung and the looping operation repeated, and so along the length

FIG. 120.—Network bag of the Yuma of Arizona. (4/8800)

HEADBAND FROM SAN JUAN RIVER, COLOMBIA. (1/2259)

143

of the headband. Thus it will be seen that the supporting threads for the beads are in a horizontal instead of a vertical position, in contrast to the Washo neck-ornament. The next line of beads is placed in the same manner, looping on to the line above it, with two beads on each side of the crossing. The bead at the point of intersection conceals the crossing and takes the place of a knot in netting. The whole weave has been accomplished line by line by attaching one to the one above. This ornament is made in an unbroken circle. The ends of the foundation cord are tied together and the looping carried around, the ends tied, and the knots neatly concealed between the beads. A finishing edge is provided by a string of beads attached to the last row of loops, in a manner corresponding to the first line along the top edge. The band is two and a quarter inches wide, and is made long enough to fit snugly a normal adult head.

A bag collected from the Yuma of Arizona (fig. 120) shows further variation. Like the specimen from Colombia, this is woven with horizontal threads, but with the difference that the strings do not loop

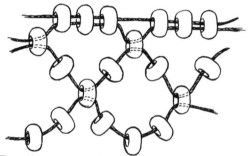

Fig. 121.—Detail of the technique of the Yuma network bag.

over the foundation cord. Fig 121 is a diagram of the system showing the use of a double string for the foundation with beads threaded on in groups of three, with both strings passing through, then one bead on one string only. The single beads placed on one string drop below the line of the three beads on both strings, as may be seen in the drawing. The network is attached to the single beads of the foundation in the manner also shown. The meshes, it will be observed, are small, having only one bead between the points where the meshes come together. There is a band about three-quarters of an inch wide around the mouth of the bag, woven in this manner. Below this is another band of about the same width, with two beads between the points of intersection, which increase the size of the mesh. The remaining portion of the netting is made with three beads between the points, which, of course, still further enlarge the mesh. A short carrying-strap is provided for the bag; this is made in the same manner as the top row of beading. The drawing shows the beads spread apart; but when they are brought together in proper position they present a closely woven appearance, not at all suggestive of network, which does not show until the meshes have been enlarged by the additional beads.

FIG. 122.—Netted collar of the Mohave. (9/70).

Another example of beaded network, from the Mohave in Arizona, is shown in fig. 122. In this instance the supporting strings for the beads are vertical, doubled over a foundation cord with two beads between the crossings (fig. 123). A band about an inch and a quarter wide is made of meshes with one bead between the points; the remaining width has the meshes extended by the use of two beads. A fringe along the lower edge is made by beading about an inch of the vertical strings and tying the ends together in pairs, with a large globular bead over the knots.

An exquisite example of the vertical string technique was collected from the Mono at Lone Pine, Inyo County, California (Pl. XXX). The foundation in this case is a band of square weave, the detail of

which is shown in fig. 87. The vertical strings are cast over the selvage edge of the band. The first four rows of meshes are supplied with three beads between the points of intersection of the meshes, but the meshes following are gradually increased in number until the bottom rows have ten and eleven beads be-

FIG. 123.—Detail of the technique of the netted Mohave collar shown in fig. 122. (9/70).

tween the points, making a mesh of one inch from point to point when extended to its greatest length. The lower edge is fringed by beading about three-quarters of an inch of the ends of the vertical strings; the upper edge is ornamented with pendants of haliotis-shell on beaded strings.

Neck-ornaments of the vertical-string type have been collected from several tribes of Nicaragua and Panama. With these peoples the foundation consists of a single t h r e a d , beaded its entire length, alternating beads being used to support the vertical threads (fig. 124). Geometric designs are woven into these variations of a net-like weave by the insertion of beads of contrasting colors at regular intervals.

FIG. 124.—Single-string foundation of beadwork from Nicaragua and Panama. (13/7624).

A necklace of netted weave between two parallel lines was collected from the Indians on Rio Napo, Department of Oriente, Ecuador. The detail drawing (fig. 125) shows a weaving of six strings which are first gathered in pairs and a few beads threaded. Then they are divided into a series of single strands; the two outer ones retain their position, while the four between are woven di-

ELABORATE SHOULDER ORNAMENT OF NETTED BEADWORK. MONO OF INYO COUNTY, CALIFORNIA. (11/8742)

agonally across, forming a net-like fabric with beads inserted at the intersections, where the knots of netting would be made. The crossing strings are passed through beads which are threaded on the two outer parallel threads at regular intervals. The drawing indicates the direction of the threads and the positions of the beads; the spaces are exaggerated to show the technique more clearly. The completed end is finished by gathering the six strands into pairs as at the beginning, with a few beads threaded to hold the pairs together. The loose ends of the threads are of sufficient length to be made into three-strand braids at each end of the weave for use as tie-strings. A design is made by the insertion of various colored beads at measured intervals. The specimen is half an inch in width.

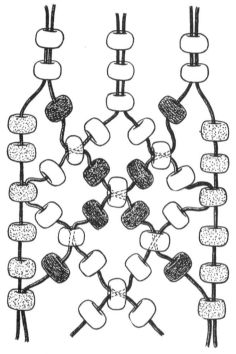

Fig. 125.—Detail of netted necklace from Rio Napo, Ecuador. (1/1764).

Examples of the same technique have been found among the Chokoi Indians of Panama.

A necklace composed of white glass beads was collected from the Akawai Indians on Essequibo river, British Guiana. The technique of the weave is very simple, as the drawing indicates (fig. 126). The two rows of twining strands lengthwise of the necklace are made of loosely twisted pink-dyed wool which bears a strong resemblance to commercial yarn. This may have found favor with the Indians, as have the beads of commerce, although, according to the Museum collections from the region, commercial yarn does not occur in any similar weave. The smaller threads supporting the beads are of native fiber, closely twisted. The mode of operation was not recorded by the collector, but it may be surmised that the two strands were

EXAMPLE OF OVERLAID OR SPOT STITCH ON A DELAWARE SHOULDER STRAP. (7/5687)

149

attached to a support of some kind, such as a pole stuck in the ground, a common device among aboriginal weavers. The beads were apparently strung and passed between the strands of yarn, and the yarn

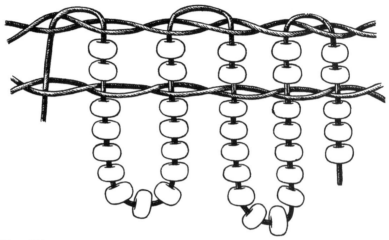

Fig. 126.—Detail of technique of a beaded necklace from British Guiana. (7/5043).

twisted after each loop of beads. No particular care was taken while making the looped fringe, as there are ten to fifteen beads to a loop; but there are always two beads between the rows of yarn. The ends of the yarn were used as tie-strings.

SEWING TECHNIQUES

Two distinct methods of sewing beads for the purpose of entirely covering broad surfaces have been employed by Indians, and each has a wide distribution. These are known as the *overlaid* or *spot stitch*, and the *lazy stitch*. In many instances, examples of both types have been collected from a single group of beadworkers.

The first of these methods, and the one having by far the wider distribution, has been employed by practically all Indian beadworkers. By its means it has been possible to produce any of the patterns that the esthetic taste of the Indians might suggest, either the graceful curving floral designs so beautifully executed by the Woodland tribes or the severely geometrical ornamentation so typical of the Siouan group. This method, termed the overlaid or spot stitch, has been used for covering broad surfaces in mass, where the leather or cloth to which the beads are attached is entirely concealed, or for the very delicate line-work shown in the admirable example illustrated in pl. XXXIII. In this technique the beads are threaded on a string and laid in the desired position, following the lines of the pattern when an overlaid stitch is made between a number of beads, sometimes two or three, or, as in a few cases, between each pair. The latter, however, occurs only in an exceptionally fine piece of work or where some very short turns in the lines of decoration are made. The overlaid stitch passes over the string on which the beads are threaded (fig. 127), and

FIG. 127.—Detail of the overlaid or spot stitch. The dotted lines show where the sewing thread turns under the surface of the material receiving the decoration.

through the surface only, if the material being decorated is leather; but if the material is cloth, the stitches are carried through from front to back. Thus the string of beads is sewed to the material. If a broad surface is to be covered, line after line is attached, the lines laid close together. The design is executed first and the background filled in afterward.

The second method has been termed the lazy stitch. In this form of decoration the beads are applied in a series of bands, each com-posed of transverse strings of beads. In this instance (fig. 128) there are seven beads to a string, but the number varies according to the artist's taste and requirement to fit the decoration in mind. Varying colors may be introduced, so arranged as to produce a design. The fig-ure illustrates the manner of sewing the beads to the article being decorated. Should it be

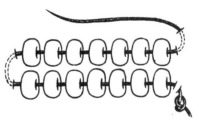

FIG. 128.—Detail of the lazy stitch. The dotted lines indicate the turn of the thread under the surface of the material being decorated.

leather, a thread either of sinew or of some other fiber, with a knotted end, was passed through a perforation in the surface of the material; if cloth was to be decorated, the stitches went through the fabric from front to back. Following this, the requisite number of beads are threaded and another stitch made, so that the beads may lay flat, at the same time being crowded close together on the string. The stitch is made at a right angle to the row of beads, emerging at the

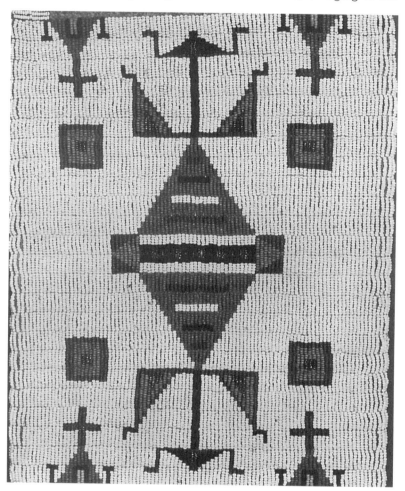

Fig. 129.—Example of the "lazy stitch" on a panel of a Sioux beaded pipe-bag. (1144).

point where the next row of beads is to be laid, which in this technique are always close together. This next row is laid in the same manner as the first, as are the succeeding rows side by side. The result is a band of solid beadwork about three-quarters of an inch

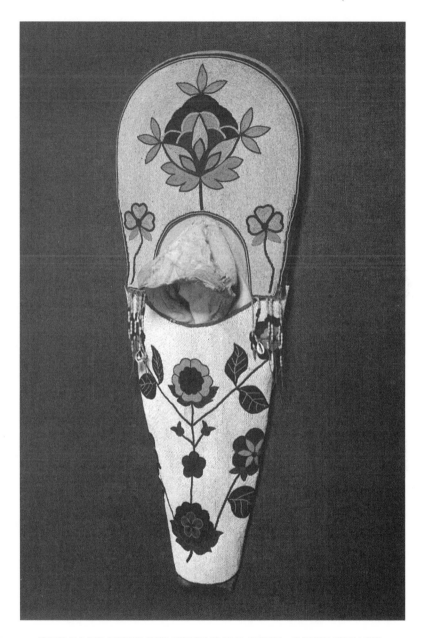

KUTENAI BABY CARRIER WITH BEADED FLORAL DESIGN. (14/3521) 37½″ LONG.

(See inside back cover for color version.)

GIRL'S COAT FROM THE ESKIMO OF THE WEST COAST OF HUDSON BAY.
(6/7302) 15″ x 30″

(See front cover for color version.)

OTH LEGGINGS OF THE CHIPPEWA DECORATED WITH SILK APPLIQUÉ OUTLINED WITH LINES OF BEADS.
(13/5900) 27" LONG

(See inside back cover for color version.)

POMO BASKET OF COILED WEAVE WITH GLASS BEADS INTERWOVEN. (4/8782) 9½" DIAMETER

(See back cover for color version.)

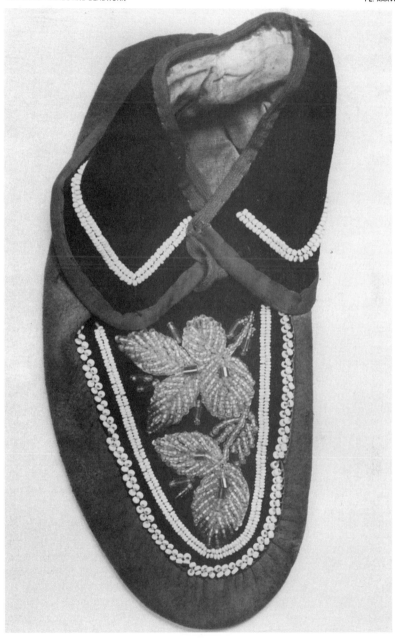

CAUGHNAWAGA MOCCASIN DECORATED WITH BEADWORK
THE LEAVES ON THE INSTEP ARE OF TRANSPARENT GLASS BEADS. (1/6925)

153

wide, more or less according to the number of beads to a row. Thus the embroidery is built up in bands which present a striking contrast to the work produced by means of the overlaid stitch. The sewing may be done with a needle, or, as is often the case when a sinew thread is used, the pointed and stiffened end of the moistened sinew follows a perforation made with an awl. Nearly all the objects of leather thus decorated are sewed with sinew. A design is introduced by spacing and counting the beads, sometimes according to a pattern marked on the leather, but more frequently without.

Illustrations of the two techniques are shown in Pl. XXXI and fig. 129. It will be seen that the lazy stitch has a well-defined ribbed effect, owing to the disposal of the beads in short rows side by side. In contrast, where the overlaid stitch has been used to cover a surface, the lines of beads are continuous and in some instances follow the shape of the design.

An attempt was made to trace the distribution of these two techniques. The materials in the Museum collection indicate that the use of the overlaid stitch prevailed among all beadworkers of the North American continent, whereas the lazy stitch was confined largely to the region west of the Mississippi, extending only a little north of the Canadian boundary. Specimens of both techniques, however, have been collected from the Loucheux of Canada. This distribution must not be taken as conclusive, for a definitive statement can be made only after an examination of all available specimens of North American beadwork, which would scarcely be possible at this time. There is, however, a variety of lazy stitch found in the East which we feel justified in classifying under another head. This I have called the *raised technique*. The sewing is practically the same as that of the lazy stitch proper, the difference being in the stringing of the beads, which may be described as follows:

The technique employed in this work is such that the pattern is raised and not sewed flat to the basic material as is ordinarily the case with beadwork. The designs are mostly of a floral nature and are especially adaptable to this type of ornamentation, by which some very beautiful specimens have been produced. The raised portions are sometimes as much as half an inch above the material to which the beads have been sewed, but the average is about a quarter of an inch. A cut-paper pattern of the leaves and flowers with their stems is first firmly sewed to the material. A commercial thread, or, in some cases, a thread of native make, is used for sewing both the

RAISED BEADWORK APPLIED TO BIRCH-BARK BY THE MOHEGAN. (3/5657, 8/7888)

patterns and the beads. The raised effect is produced by first attaching the thread to the starting point on the pattern. If that should be a leaf, the midrib would normally be selected. More than a sufficient number of beads to fill the length of the midrib are placed on the thread, which is then caught into the material and the edge of the paper pattern. There being more beads on the thread than necessary for the length of the midrib, they form an arc between the two points of contact with the pattern. The veins of the leaves being worked out in the same manner from the midrib to the edge of the leaf, a raised or looped effect is produced, which in some cases is very realistic. The lines of beads are all so close together that it is not possible for any of the loops to lie over to one side. The stems or single lines are all more or less flat. Transparent colorless glass beads have been used to some extent in this technique, particularly in the older specimens; otherwise many specimens show the use of opaque beads of many tints.

This particular form of decoration is usually applied to a background of cloth, and the paper pattern no doubt was considered to be the easiest and most practical way to lay out the design to be beaded. Black cloth seems to have been preferred, and when transparent beads were used the paper lent more body to the color of the decoration. Most specimens of this technique in the Museum collections were obtained from the Caughnawaga and Tuscarora. Judging by the apparent age of some of the work, this form of decoration was adopted during the early stages of beadwork. Other specimens have been collected from the Mohawk, Cayuga, Onondaga, and Mohegan, and some closely related work has come from the Penebscot. Pl. XXXVI illustrates a moccasin of Caughnawaga origin having an instep piece with leaf and tendril design wrought in transparent glass beads. The bordering lines are white opaque beads, the inner line is composed of two rows or strings of beads which are attached to the foundation at irregular intervals by a crossing stitch (fig. 127), as in the case of the edging around the ankle flap. The outer edge of the instep is trimmed with pairs of beads attached with a diagonally crossing stitch.

Fig. 130 portrays a pouch, bearing the same form of decoration, collected from the Grand River Iroquois in Canada. The beads are of opaque glass. The double-row edging is applied as in the case of the Caughnawaga moccasin. The detail of the beading on the edge of the flap to the left in the illustration is shown in fig. 131.

Examples of raised technique are shown in Pl. XXXVII, in which the beads are attached to birch-bark with a paper foundation, in the manner that such ornamentation has been applied to cloth. The use of birch-bark for this purpose, however, is unique, and so far specimens of this kind have been obtained only from the Mohegan. The

Fig. 130.—Beaded pouch of the Iroquois of Grand River reservation, Canada. (1/6947).

objects illustrated are fragmentary and are probably parts of trinket boxes.[48]

Bead-ornamented garments made by the Eskimo are not common. The most highly decorated pieces have been obtained from the region of Chesterfield inlet on the west coast of Hudson bay. Pl. XXXIII

[48] See Speck, F. G., Northern Elements in Iroquois and New England Art, *Indian Notes,* vol. II, no. 1, 1925.

illustrates a hooded coat of a Kenipitumiut Eskimo girl of that territory.[49] According to Low, the Aivillingmiut, who occupy the country northward of Chesterfield inlet, are the Eskimo who came in closer contact with American whalers, hence, as might be expected, their art, among other phases of their life, has been more or less modified by civilization. The art of beadwork may have spread to the south from these people. A woman's elaborately beaded coat recently acquired by the Museum is said to have been obtained from the Padlimiut, who occupy a wide territory, including Rankin inlet, southward to Churchill river and westward to Dubawant lake. Capt. George Comer, a whaler who has made extensive collections of ethnological material and data from the Eskimo of the west coast of Hudson bay, says that such garments are the most cherished of all their possessions and are worn only on special occasions. Captain Comer also says that beads were introduced into that region by Parry and Lyon during their search for a northwest passage in 1821–22 and that he saw some beads in possession of one of the natives that had been originally obtained from those explorers and which had been handed down from mother to daughter.

The technique employed in the beadwork of this region is the overlaid stitch; that is, the beads are strung and attached to the garment with a stitch cast over the thread on which the beads are strung. In addition there is a quantity of beaded fringe, some with looped ends and others with pendants of small caribou-teeth.

An exceptionally good example of fine-line beading is shown in the pair of Chippewa leggings illustrated in Pl. XXXIV. They are made of broadcloth of the kind that found favor among the Indians in their early trade with the whites. The decoration consists of a somewhat conventionalized floral design of silk appliqué in a variety of colors outlined with delicate lines of beads. This is an instance in which European materials exclusively were used very effectively by the Indians to express their esthetic sense without the introduction of even a suggestion of European ideas as to design or color. The combination of color and design is truly artistic, and may be classed among the best specimens of the kind in the Museum collections. The beads are first strung and then attached to the leggings by an overlaid stitch (fig. 127).

---

[49] The name of this group is recorded by Low, A. P., The Cruise of the Neptune, Ottawa, 1906, p. 135.

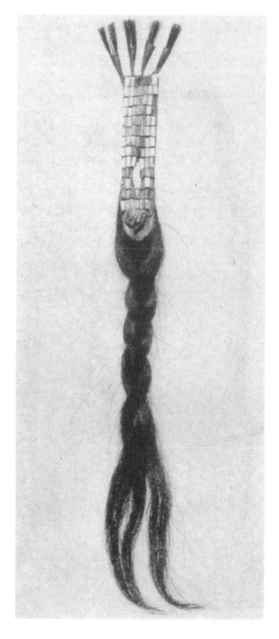

IOWA INDIAN HAIR-ORNAMENT MADE FROM A BUFFALO-TAIL, DECORATED WITH WAMPUM
BEADS. FROM A SACRED BUNDLE
(Courtesy of the Milwaukee Public Museum)

Pl. XXXVIII is a specimen in the collection of the Milwaukee Public Museum, showing an unusual use of wampum. It consists of a hair-ornament made of a bison's tail, which was part of the paraphernalia found in an Iowa buffalo doctor's bundle. The hide has been spread out, roughly tanned, and decorated with thirteen rows of wampum, originally seven beads in each row, with the exception that near the lower end the hide has been perforated for some purpose, and here in three rows only six beads each were used. The unusual feature is that the beads have been sewed directly to the leather with a sinew thread, instead of being woven together and then fastened in place. This is the only specimen so far brought to notice where wampum beads have been so used. Several of the beads are missing, but enough remain to reveal the fact that a pattern has been worked with purple and white, consisting of a band of dark beads, three beads wide, down the center, and two cross-bands at the lower end. The whole has been smeared with blue paint.

EDGINGS

Many articles made of leather or cloth have been embellished with a beaded edging regardless of whether the surface has been ornamented or not. Fig. 131 illustrates an almost universal type. As the drawing shows, the thread is passed through a bead, then through the edge of the material, and up through the bead again. Another bead is

FIG. 131.—Detail of two-beaded edging. (2/1129).

threaded, and the thread is made to go through still another bead before passing through the material. By this arrangement there are beads in alternating positions, vertical and horizontal, only the latter being sewed directly to the edge. This form of ornamentation has been applied not only to clothing, but to all kinds of objects to which some form of decoration could be attached.

FIG. 132.—Detail of single-beaded edging. Tahltan.

A less common method is shown in fig. 132, which is found more frequently on specimens from the Northwest than elsewhere. The Tahltan have employed it to a great extent in ornamenting their gambling-stick bags, knife-sheaths,

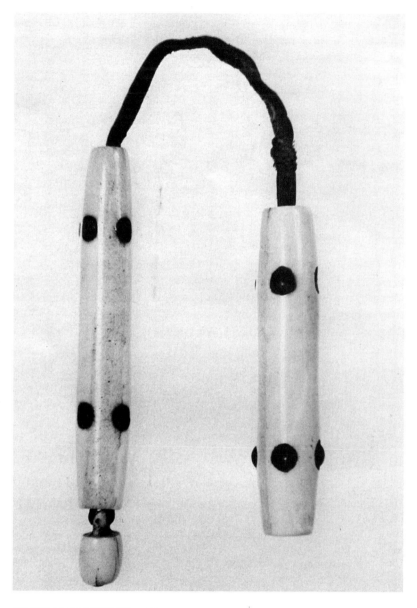

NEEDLE-CASES OF WALRUS-IVORY INLAID WITH SECTIONS OF BEADS. ESKIMO OF POINT BARROW, ALASKA. (3/4703)

and pouches. As will be seen in the drawing, a single row of beads only is used, and the thread crosses itself between the beads. In both drawings the beads are purposely spread apart in order to show the movement of the threads. In the finished work the threads are hardly visible.

An uncommon form of line-work is illustrated in fig. 133. Instead of a single row of beads such as is commonly employed for line decoration, two rows of beads are used

Fig. 133.—Detail of two-beaded line-work.

with a looping stitch. The dotted lines in the drawing show the position of the threads under the cloth. This technique has not been found on leather. The solid lines indicate the position of the thread looped above and passing through the beads. This technique has been used by the Alibamu, Choctaw, and Koasati, with some very pleasing results. Circles and scrolls are the dominating features of their designs.

BEAD INLAYS

Uses for glass beads for ornamentation other than the usual methods of stringing, weaving, or sewing them, have been found. The Eskimo of Alaska have decorated many of their objects with bead inlays. Among these may be mentioned the bead labrets once commonly worn by the Eskimo on the Alaskan mainland and the islands northward from Kuskokwim river.

Nelson [50] has described the method of making and preparing a hole for the reception of a labret:

The hole is made just below each corner of the mouth and at first a long, thin, nail-like plug of ivory, about an inch in length, having a slight enlargement at the inner end, is thrust through the opening and left for some time. After the wearer becomes accustomed to this a somewhat larger plug . . . is inserted in the hole for the purpose of enlarging it. This process is repeated, a larger plug being used on each occasion until the hole is of the size desired. In many cases the hole is so large that the teeth are visible through the opening when the labret is not in place.

The increasing contact with civilization has rendered this form of decoration almost obsolete. Fig. 134 represents a labret from the

[50] Nelson, E. W., The Eskimo about Bering Strait, *Eighteenth Ann. Rep. Bur. Amer. Ethnol., 1896–97,* pt. 1, p. 48, Washington, 1899.

Eskimo of Point Barrow, Alaska, made of walrus ivory with half of a large blue-glass bead set in the center of the disc. This type was used by the men. The woman's labret was a small sickle-shape object with a small flat button on one end to hold it in place. When two of these were worn they were sometimes connected with a string of glass beads across the chin.

FIG. 134.—Labret of walrus-ivory with bead inlay. Eskimo of Point Barrow, Alaska. (10/8284).

Two needle-cases made of walrus ivory are illustrated in Pl. XXXIX, which are ornamented with pieces of beads inlaid. The beads have been split in two along the perforation, and the half-sections, inserted in cavities made for their reception, are secured with some kind of glue. The harmony of color makes these two objects very attractive. This form of decoration is applied by the Eskimo to numerous articles. In addition to those illustrated there are hunting and fishing charms, mouth-pieces for drills, and dolls, of both ivory and wood. In the case of the dolls, the beads are used for the eyes, usually a white bead of suitable size so set that the perforation represents the pupil. Carvings of animals in wood and ivory are sometimes treated in the same manner.

The Indians of California have contributed many specimens showing the use of beads for inlaying. Invariably these are small discoidal shell beads and are applied to objects of stone, bone, and shell. Many of these have already been fully described.[51]

An example of shell ornaments decorated with small discoidal beads so common to California is shown in fig. 135. A number of stone rings of problematical use have received the same form of decoration, as have mortars and pestles; and many bone flutes and whistles have been similarly treated. In all these objects the disc beads have been cemented in place with bitumen.

The Huichol Indians of Mexico have produced some remarkable specimens of bead-ornamented objects, most of which were designed for use in religious ceremonies. Carvings of wood representing animals, tablets of wood, bowls made from gourds, and numerous other things intended as votive offerings, are all more or less covered with elaborate designs in beads of various colors embedded in a thick coating of beeswax.

---

[51] Heye, G. G., Certain Aboriginal Artifacts from San Miguel Island, California, *Indian Notes and Monographs*, vol. VII, no. 4, 1921.

Pl. XXXX illustrates two gourd bowls, one with a conventional floral design, the other with figures representing deer. Some of the beads were strung before being pressed into the wax, others were placed

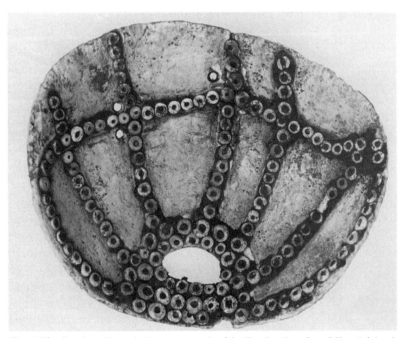

Fig. 135.—Lævicardium shell ornamented with disc beads. San Miguel island, California. (9/4907).

one by one. The ceremonies associated with these objects have been described by Lumholtz.[52]

A collection of pottery figures in human and animal forms have been added to the Museum collections from the Carib Indians of Dutch Guiana. These are said to have been made for use in the survival of an old ceremony whose significance is now practically lost. However, a great deal of care has been exercised in the manufacture of the figures, for in addition to their decoration with painted designs, they are supplied with glass beads for eyes.

BEADED BASKETS

Bead decoration on baskets is fairly common among some of the basket-making tribes of California. This style of ornamentation was

---

[52] Lumholtz, Carl, Symbolism of the Huichol Indians, *Mem. Amer. Mus. Nat. Hist.*, vol. iii, New York, 1900.

VOTIVE BOWLS MADE FROM GOURDS AND INCRUSTED WITH GLASS BEADS. HUICHOL INDIANS, MEXICO. (11/9488, 11/9489).

not confined to the use of glass beads of commerce, for in the Museum collections there are many excellent specimens of baskets on which shell beads of native manufacture have been used. Pl. XXXV, however, shows the use of glass beads for this purpose. This specimen, of Pomo origin, is of the typical coil weave, with a single-rod foundation.[53]

A better understanding of the method of applying beads in this form of decoration will be gained from a brief description of the basket technique. The " single-rod foundation " consists of a rod of willow or of other flexible material, shaved to a uniform diameter and of size according to requirements. Commencing at the bottom of the basket the rod is bent around spirally, and the spirals sewed together with some other flexible material, such as roots of plants or the soft stems of willow or rhus, which when thoroughly soaked in water are so pliable that the rod foundation may be entirely concealed. The sewing is a wrapping or " coiling." The stitch passes around the rod and is caught into or under the coiling of the adjoining spirals as the weave progresses. As the basket grows in the making, additional rods are spliced with an even joint to the preceding ones. Some of the work is so fine and the materials are drawn together so closely that a well-woven basket is practically water-tight. The design on the specimen illustrated was produced by the use of black coiling material in contrast to the light-colored material forming the rest of the weave. The pattern has been further emphasized by the application of dark-colored beads, while white beads have been incorporated in the coils of the background by passing a strand of the coiling material through one bead at each stitch.

In most cases where shell beads have been used they are sewn to the basket after completion of the weaving, as an auxiliary ornamentation. More often, however, they were used as an edging at the rim or were strung and used as handles.

A very unusual specimen of beaded basketry is from the Nootka of Vancouver island. It is made of cedar-bark splints of the checker weave, in which the warp and weft are of the same width, crossing one another at right angles, one over and one under. Large so-called Russian beads of dark-blue glass have been threaded on the elements at somewhat irregular intervals (fig. 136). A design has been woven into the basket with strips of bark dyed red and black. The rim is

---

[53] See Mason, O. T., Aboriginal American Basketry, *Rep. U. S. Nat. Mus. for 1902*, Washington, 1904.

ornamented with rows of beads, one red and the other blue, sewed on with a thread in the manner shown in fig. 133.

Fig. 136.—Nootka basket made of cedar bark with glass beads interwoven. (6/3341).

Art in beadwork, like other means employed to give expression to the esthetic side of Indian life, is fast yielding to the encroachment of civilization. In a measure the trader's influence is responsible for the perceptible decline. Very often objects are produced solely for trade, and often with designs whose meaning is entirely lost. Indeed it is frequently the case that meaningless patterns have been devised, sometimes at the suggestion of traders; consequently genuine native art in bead embroidery with its designs so replete with meaning and significance is rarely produced today. Not alone in this respect is the finer work becoming scarce, but in the haste to supply the commercial demand the excellent workmanship so characteristic of earlier times is now almost unknown.

More regrettable still is the fact that the religious activities of the Indians, which, as with other peoples, have done so much to stimulate their art expression, are sadly misrepresented and discouraged. With a new mode of living forced upon the Indians, the day is not far distant when distinctively aboriginal American art will be a thing of the past.

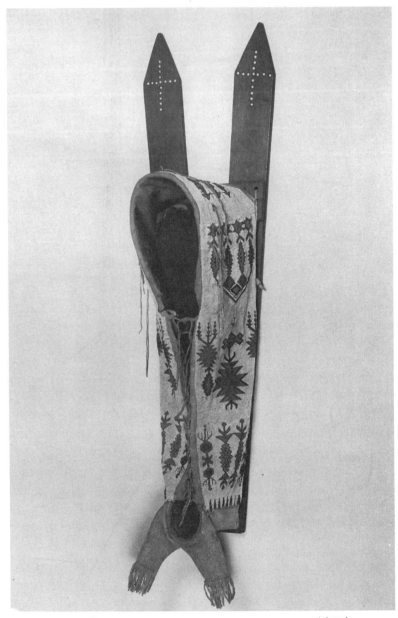

COMANCHE CRADLE WITH WOVEN BEADWORK DECORATION. (5/7467)